DONNELLEY AND THE YELLOW PAGES

The Birth
of An Advertising
Medium

DONNELLEY AND THE YELLOW PAGES

The Birth
of An Advertising
Medium

BETTYE H. PRUITT

Bettye H. Pruitt holds a Ph.D. in history from Boston University and is Consultant at The Winthrop Group, Inc., in Cambridge, Massachusetts.

FOREWORD

In 1886, a young 22-year-old Chicagoan Reuben Hamilton Donnelley published the classified directory of the Chicago Telephone Company.

It was a modest beginning, but an inspired one. During his life's course, also the formative years of his company, Donnelley strove to maintain the highest ethical practices, the clearest regard for his employees, and the type of innovative leadership that would propel the company to the forefront of the Yellow Pages directory industry.

As we look back over the first hundred years, the strength of the Donnelley organization is a living testimony, not only to that one man, but to all who have contributed so much in his path.

Our company growth has been unmatched, our search for innovative solutions unsurpassed, and our commitment to excellence unwavering.

As we enter our second century of excellence, innovation, and service we remain steadfast in our purpose to find better ways to meet the needs of directory users and advertisers, buyers and sellers.

Our sincere appreciation goes to our employees and to our customers.

The Donnelley Centennial is a tribute to you.

Kenneth O. Johnson
President
Donnelley Directory

William Bak
President
Donnelley Information Publishing

Richard B. Swank
Executive Vice President
The Dun & Bradstreet Corporation

PREFACE

Writing the history of any company that can look back over 100 years is a worthwhile task, but the history of the Reuben H. Donnelley Corporation—now Donnelley Directory/Donnelley Information Publishing—has a number of unique aspects to recommend it. There is no published history of the Yellow Pages industry, although this ubiquitous and indispensable reference book has surely played a vital role in shaping 20th-century American society. Reuben Donnelley's career as a pioneer and successful entrepreneur in classified directory publishing illuminates its origins and early development.

Moreover, within two decades of Donnelley's death in 1929, his company expanded to become the largest independent publisher and sales agent for Bell System directories. Conforming to systemwide standards as these developed, Donnelley also took the lead at various times with innovations and improvements of its own devising. Thus its story is very much a part of the mainstream of historical development in the directory industry.

For a century, this enterprise has enjoyed continuous, often astonishing growth, directly attributable to the fact that its fortunes were closely tied to those of the telephone industry and, through directory advertising, to the expanding U.S. consumer economy. Yet, while its status as a monopoly within a monopoly remained unchanged for 64 years, Donnelley underwent significant internal changes and passed through several distinct phases in its relationship with AT&T. The most dramatic of these changes came in waves of managerial reform, beginning about 1950 and culminating on the eve of divestiture, around 1980, each aimed at improving sales performance and boosting revenue gains above the rate of growth enjoyed throughout the System. The story of this long period of transformation is a valuable chapter in American business history, one that sheds some light on the subtle workings of competition within a large-scale monopoly, the only one of its kind to survive so far into the 20th century.

The Donnelley directory organization will begin its 101st year in a business environment far more similar to what Reuben Donnelley experienced than to the recent past. Its split into two companies, one to provide sales and publishing services under contract and one to publish proprietary directories, reflects the radical disjuncture that has occurred in the directory industry. In the aggressive posture it has assumed since the reopening of competition, Donnelley can draw strength from the legacy of its founder's entrepreneurism. Yet the foundation of its present position rests squarely on the leadership it has enjoyed over the past 30 years. While it seems certain that Donnelley's second century will scarcely resemble the first, whatever future success it is to enjoy will be firmly rooted in its long history of adaptation and growth.

ACKNOWLEDGEMENTS

I wish to thank all of those people within Donnelley who assisted me in the research for this history. Erik H. Rambusch, Director of Human Resources, orchestrated the project, contributing a great deal of his time and energy, as well as his own insight and ideas. Jan F. Cremer, in King of Prussia, and Grace M. Langan, in Chicago, were both extremely helpful in sending me their archives of company publications; Shirley Juris helped me to locate and use materials in the office at Purchase and in the corporate archives in Spring Valley, New York. Special thanks are also due to the many Donnelley executives, both current and retired, who gave several hours of their time for interviews, without which this work would have been impossible. Their names are listed at the conclusion of this book, following the reference notes. I am also grateful to Tibor Taraba, Director of Communications at Donnelley, for shepherding the manuscript to published form. Last but not least, I wish to acknowledge the contribution of my colleague, David Grayson Allen, who conducted many of the interviews and played a major role in shaping the analysis presented here.

TABLE OF CONTENTS

I
Chicago Origins
(1864–1886)

Reuben H. Donnelley was born in Hamilton, Ontario, in August 1864, just two months before his parents moved to Chicago, then the very heart of the developing United States. Here Reuben's father, Richard R. Donnelley, established himself as a printer and publisher, laying the foundation of what would become one of the largest printing companies in the world. Later, Reuben would take over one part of his father's business, directory publishing, and transform it into a new industry—telephone directory advertising.

Prosperous, populous Chicago was fertile ground for such enterprise. In 1836, when Reuben's father was born, the population of Chicago had been about 4,000. One visitor to Chicago in the mid-1840s described it as "raw and bare, standing on its high prairie above the lake shore." But it was the penultimate boom town, "the mushroom metropolis of the West," that would be transformed within half a century "from a trading post on the bank of a muddy creek to one of the world's greatest cities."[1] By the time the Donnelley family arrived in Chicago, its population had grown to 185,000. During the 65 years of Reuben's lifetime it reached 3.3 million, and the North Central region of the United States, of which Chicago was the center, reigned as the most populous in the nation. Chicago in these years enjoyed unparalleled economic growth as commerce and industry expanded to keep pace with the demands of the growing city, region, and nation.[2]

Chicago's location made it the central entrepot for the industrializing nation. The completion of the Erie Canal in 1824 linked it, via the Great Lakes and the Hudson River, to the Atlantic seaboard. In 1849, the Illinois and Michigan Canal made a connection with the Mississippi River, and in the same year the new Galena & Chicago Union Railroad brought in its first load of wheat from the Des Plaines River. "Chicago had become Chicago," and quickly it became the largest wheat and corn market in the nation. By 1856 it had 10 railroad trunk lines with 58 passenger trains and 38 freight trains arriving and departing daily. At the same time as many as 300 ships passed into and out of Chicago's harbor each day. In the year that the Donnelleys arrived, over 10 million bushels of wheat came into the city, mostly by rail, and were shipped out across the Great Lakes. Some 500 million feet of lumber cane down the Lakes, and 300 million feet went out by rail and across the Canal to the Mississippi. The city was the middleman, delivering food to the growing urban population of the East and sending out the lumber needed to build the houses, barns, and shops of the Midwest.[3]

This hub of commerce was a logical place for the location of industry, and in the late 1860s, Chicago began to establish its preeminence as a manufacturing city. In addition to lumber, it began to import finished wood products such as wagons, ships, and even a complete line of prefabricated buildings—"cottages, villas, school houses, stores, taverns, churches, court-houses, or towns, wholesale and retail . . . securely packed, to any part of the country." Cyrus McCormick's factory produced 10,000 McCormick reapers per annum, which it sold throughout America and Europe. The first Chicago meat-packing plant had been opened by Archibald Clybourne in 1829; 25 years later, the city was exporting some 25,000 tons of cured meats annually. The opening of the Union Stock Yards in 1865 sealed Chicago's title as "The Great Bovine City of the World." In the same year, the North Chicago Rolling Mills produced the nation's first steel rail, laying the foundation for Chicago's later leadership as a steel producer. Many smaller industries flourished as well, and, within less than a decade following the Civil War, the city transformed a trade deficit of 140 million pounds of "merchandise and sundries" into a trade surplus of 254 million pounds.[4]

The Donnelleys arrived in Chicago seven months before the end of the war. Three years earlier, Richard Donnelley had left an established position as a partner in the newspaper firm of the New Orleans *True Delta* because of his unwillingness to support the Confederate cause. Although he still wanted to practice his trade in the U.S., he had returned to his native Canada and to his home town of Hamilton, where he established a printing firm in partnership with Joseph Lawson. In 1863, he married Naomi Ann Shenstone, the daughter of a Baptist minister in nearby Brantford, Ontario. Soon after, Donnelley heard of an opportunity in the Chicago publishing firm of Church & Goodman and was able to buy into this business. When they arrived in Chicago, the only lodging the Donnelley family could find was on Michigan Avenue, an area filled with Confederate sympathizers. Soon, however, they were able to move to Wabash Avenue, a more congenial neighborhood.[5]

Richard Donnelley, the Reverend Mr. Leroy Church, and Edward

Goodman began their association on common ground. Both Donnelley & Lawson in Canada and Church & Goodman in Chicago had specialized in religious publications. However, as one of only a few printing and publishing firms in Chicago in the 1860s, the new partnership quickly expanded into other areas. Within a few years they were publishing a wide variety of periodicals in addition to books and magazines such as *The Christian Times* and *The Witness,* published previously by Church & Goodman. They also printed works published by others, including the *The Annual Report of the Chicago Board of Education.* Soon they became one of the largest printing and publishing firms west of Philadelphia.

In 1868, they acquired new quarters at 108–110 Dearborn Street, and the publishing and printing parts of the business were separated. Church & Goodman, Publishers, hung their sign over an office on the ground floor, while Church, Goodman, & Donnelley, Steam Printers, announced themselves as the occupants of the floor above. Two years later, this separation became complete with the dissolution of Church, Goodman & Donnelley and the incorporation of The Lakeside Publishing and Printing Company. The name "Lakeside" was chosen to echo the name of the Riverside Press of Cambridge, Massachusetts, which Donnelley hoped to emulate. He became manager of the new company, and Church served as its president, although Church & Goodman continued to operate independently as publishers. As the crowning touch to seven years of prosperity and growth, plans were drawn up for an imposing Gothic-style structure, the Lakeside Building, that would house all the machinery and staff necessary to the printing and publishing business.[6]

The Chicago Fire

Then catastrophe struck the young company. Exactly one year after its incorporation, the entire Lakeside Publishing and Printing Company, including the unfinished Lakeside Building, was in ashes, swept away by the great Chicago Fire that raged through the city on October 8–9, 1871. The period of prosperity and rapid advancement that they had enjoyed since 1864 had come to an end, but Donnelley refused to accept defeat. His good credit and reputation enabled him to reestablish himself almost

---

1864: *Reuben H. Donnelley is born in August, in Hamilton, Ontario, to Richard R. and Naomi Ann Shenstone Donnelley . . . The Democratic Party meets in Chicago, nominating General George B. McClellan for President . . . Admiral David G. Farragut leads a Union fleet of 18 ships against Mobile Bay; Alabama's USS Tecumseh is torpedoed and sinks . . . Charles Dickens publishes* Our Mutual Friend, *his first full-length novel.*

immediately as "R. R. Donnelley, Steam Printer." Two years later, with the financial backing of a real estate broker, W. L. Peck, he was able to reestablish the Lakeside Publishing and Printing Company and even to rebuild the planned Lakeside Building on its original site.

The year 1873, however, brought a panic on the stock exchange and the beginning of a general depression. Donnelley was forced to make valiant efforts to keep the Lakeside Publishing and Printing Company alive through diversification. In 1873, he took up directory publishing, and, in 1874, he set out with Alexander Loyd to develop a line of "dime novels," inexpensive reprints of popular fiction, which they called the Lakeside Library. The Lakeside Library was soon driven out of the market by competition from the Seaside Library, published in New York, but diversification into directory publishing proved to be one of the most significant steps that Richard Donnelley took. The printing of directories became an important component of his own future prosperity, and directory publishing opened up a career path for his son, Reuben Donnelley.

The First Directories

By 1844, there were more than 10 well-established city directories around the nation. The first Chicago city directory was published in that year by James W. Norris. Its title, *The General Directory and Business Advertiser of the City of Chicago, for the Year 1844,* is suggestive of the function that the directory was designed to serve. The fact that Norris also operated a "General Intelligence and Agency Office"—an employment agency—is also significant. In the days before telegraph and telephone networks had been established within cities, businessmen relied on messengers, and business information traveled only by word of mouth or indirectly through newspapers and public notices. In this milieu, city directories provided

---

1870: *Church, Goodman and Donnelley Steam Printers becomes The Lakeside Printing and Publishing Company . . . John D. Rockefeller and others organize the Standard Oil Company of Ohio . . . Confederate General-in-Chief Robert E. Lee dies at the age of 63 . . . Virginia, Mississippi, Texas and Georgia are readmitted to the Union . . . The boardwalk at Atlantic City, New Jersey, is completed. . . .*

1873: *Richard R. Donnelley publishes a Chicago City Directory . . . President U. S. Grant begins his second term . . . William "Boss" Tweed is convicted on 102 counts of fraud . . . Mark Twain and Charles Dudley Warner collaborate on The Gilded Age . . . Yale, Princeton, Columbia and Rutgers Universities meet to draw up the first rules for football . . . Andrew Hallidee develops cable cars for the hills of San Francisco.*

Sample pages from Donnelley's Chicago Telephone Directory, 1886

*Reuben Donnelley with some members of
his staff taken about 1924*

information that was essential to business. They were compiled from information gathered by canvassers who went door to door, attempting to locate every individual by residence and occupation. In addition to the alphabetical list of inhabitants, most directory publishers put together a business directory listing firms under classified headings and offering them an opportunity to advertise their goods or services. It does not seem surprising that, in his capacity as an employment agent, Norris would have seen the need for a directory in a city such as Chicago.[7]

By the 1870s, publication of the Chicago city directory was in the hands of Richard Edwards, of Louisville, Kentucky. Edwards published directories in a number of western cities, relying on a manager in each location to handle the details. In 1872, he arranged with Richard Donnelley to take on the *Edwards Annual Directory of Chicago,* which appeared in that year with Donnelley and Edwards as publishers and The Lakeside Publishing and Printing Company as printers. In 1873, it seems that Donnelley either purchased the directory business from Edwards or started to publish his own directory in competition. For 1874 (and perhaps for 1873) one finds *The Lakeside Annual Directory of Chicago,* published by Williams, Donnelley & Company, a subsidiary of the Lakeside Publishing and Printing Company, set up to handle this business.[8]

In 1875, as business continued to contract in the depression, publication of the city directory was taken over by Donnelley, Loyd & Company, a separate subsidiary that had been established to handle publication of the Lakeside Library. When the Lakeside Library project was abandoned, the Lakeside Publishing and Printing Company itself went out of business.[9] Richard Donnelley's rise could not be stalled for long, however. Donnelley, Loyd & Company took over the printing equipment of the Lakeside Publishing and Printing Company, while ownership of the Lakeside Building reverted to the estate of the company's former benefactor, W. L. Peck. Within a year, Donnelley had found a new investor, another real estate man, Norman T. Gassette, and a new firm, Donnelley, Gassette & Loyd, Printers and Publishers, was launched in 1878. Donnelley was soon able to purchase the interests of both Loyd and Gassette, and in 1879 he became President, Treasurer, and Director of Donnelley, Gassette & Loyd. The company was reorganized as R. R. Donnelley & Sons in 1882, and it was incorporated under that name in 1890, completing Richard Donnelley's long struggle to establish a printing firm of his own in Chicago.

Richard Donnelley's craft was printing, learned in the classic way, through an apprenticeship. Yet he was continually forced to take a hand in publishing as well, as a means of creating business for his printing presses. Clear in his mind that these two functions, publishing and printing, were distinctive, requiring different skills, he strove to separate them whenever possible. Church, Goodman & Donnelley, for example, very quickly became a separate entity from Church & Goodman, Publishers. Later, when Donnelley was struggling to reestablish the Lakeside Publishing and Printing Company, he created, first, Williams; Donnelley & Co. to publish *The Edwards Chicago City Directory* and then, Donnelley, Loyd & Co. to publish the Lakeside Library. Williams, Donnelley & Co. was subsumed under Donnelley, Loyd & Co., and, after 1877, the entire business was unified within Donnelley, Gassette & Loyd. But as soon as his business fortunes improved and he began to regain controlling interest in the enterprise, Donnelley sought once again to separate the publishing and the printing functions. In 1880, he created the Chicago Directory Company to handle the publishing end of what had become by then a major part of the Donnelley business, and, by 1890, he had become what he wanted to be—a printer, and nothing more.[10]

Reuben Donnelley: Early Years

In 1880, Reuben Donnelley was in his midteens. He had graduated from Hyde Park High School and attended, briefly, the old University of Chicago. His inclinations, however, were toward business rather than scholarship, and, for this reason, he enrolled in The Bryant and Stratton Business College. He began to work as a canvasser for the Chicago Directory Company in 1881, while still in school, and joined the firm full-time a year later with the title of clerk. By 1885, he was head of the canvassing department. Thomas Hutchinson, who had worked as compiler of the *Lakeside Annual City Directory* since 1876, was President, Manager, and Chief Compiler in these years.[11]

During this early period of Reuben Donnelley's association with the Chicago Directory Company, significant advances were made in the development of the classified business directory as an advertising medium. In 1882, the company began publishing the *Lakeside Annual Business Directory,* which was a reprint of the business section of the city directory. Although the city directory was the only one in Chicago, this new book was in competition with Rand McNally & Company's *Annual Business Directory of Chicago.* By 1885, the *Lakeside Annual Business Directory* included

---

1880: *The Chicago Directory Company is created by Richard Donnelley . . . Alexander Graham Bell invents the photophone, and sends the first wireless telephone message . . . Sarah Bernhardt appears at Booth's Theatre in New York to begin her tour of* La Dame aux Camelias, *by Alexandre Dumas fils . . . Andrew Carnegie begins establishment of the Carnegie Libraries . . . Gilbert and Sullivan's comic opera* The Pirates of Penzance *opens in London after a New York premiere.*

many special features for users, perhaps intended to improve its position against Rand McNally. Under "Miscellaneous Information," it gave a classified list of all city and county offices, public institutions such as churches and libraries, physicians, and organizations such as labor unions and private clubs. It also contained a "Street and Avenue Guide," with a separate list of streets that had changed their names during the year. Finally, at the beginning of the business list, there was a nine-page "Eastern Department," listing firms from Boston, New York, Providence, Bridgeport, and Worcester.

Moving up to be head of the canvassing department during the years when this business directory was being developed, Reuben Donnelley was undoubtedly deeply involved in soliciting advertisements from Chicago businesses and probably also in devising ways to make the *Lakeside Directory* an effective competitor against Rand McNally. He was also able to learn the details of directory compilation from an experienced teacher, Thomas Hutchinson, who had been working on Chicago directories for over a decade. By 1886, he had advanced to become Assistant Manager of the company, and in the *Lakeside Annual City Directory* of that year he was listed as Assistant Compiler. At the age of 21, Reuben Donnelley had worked with city directories and directory advertising for five years, training himself to take over this all-important adjunct of his family's growing printing business. Within a year he would take over from Hutchinson as Manager and Chief Compiler.

The 1886 Chicago Telephone Directory

Early in 1886, a contract was signed between the Chicago Telephone Company and R. R. Donnelley & Sons for publication of the telephone directory three times annually. As Richard Donnelley's son and as the central figure in the Chicago Directory Company, Reuben was undoubtedly the person largely responsible for the first Donnelley telephone directory. The appearance of this directory, the *Chicago Telephone Directory* of May 15, 1886, is generally acknowledged as the birth of classified telephone directory advertising. [12]

The terms of the contract regarding the classified portion of that directory are clearly implied in the following statement, made by the Telephone Company in the front of the book:

> . . . This Company has nothing whatever to do with the insertion of advertisements or display lines in the Directory, which are the property of the publishers, and must be arranged for with them. [13]

Thus Donnelley was able to sell advertising in the telephone directory, just as he did in the city directory. The book that he produced under this contract is the prototype of what we know as the Yellow Pages.

The application of full-scale directory advertising to the list of telephone subscribers was an innovation. Moreover, it was an undertaking of some risk in the face of strong competition from the well-established city directories. Chicago, like most major cities, had had a Bell telephone directory, including a classified list of business subscribers, since 1878. Published sporadically through 1885 by the firm of J. W. Connorton, the classified section had grown from three to 76 two-column pages. This expansion reflected the rapid spread of the telephone, especially after the consolidation of the Chicago Bell Telephone Company and a competing Edison company, the American District Telegraph Company, into the Chicago Telephone Company in 1881.

But, even then, the telephone was still very far from the essential instrument of communication that it is today. For example, while there were close to a thousand "Physicians and Surgeons" listed in the *Lakeside Business Directory* of 1885–1886 only 30 had phones. Of the 200 odd "Printers, Book and Job," only 53 had phones—including both R. R. Donnelley & Sons and Rand McNally. Even in one of its largest headings, "Coal Dealers," the telephone directory had less than half the number of listings found in the annual business directory.[14]

Despite the small telephone population, it is clear that Donnelley made a significant commitment of resources to developing advertising in the telephone directory. Among the physicians, three bought boldface and extra lines to list their hours, and out of 128 listings under "Coal Dealers," there were 32 boldface, nine quarter-page ads, one half-page ad, and two full-page ads. The phone company did not take a share of the advertising revenues, but there was still no certainty that they would cover the cost of the time spent by the Chicago Directory Company canvassers in raising them. In later years, Reuben Donnelley claimed to have "started the Chicago Classified Telephone Directory, the pioneer book of its kind in the world," and he explained this achievement by the fact that he had "sensed the value of the telephone." Certainly no other telephone directory publisher strove as Donnelley did to develop advertising in the classified list, either then or for many years thereafter.[15]

1882: *The firm of Donnelley, Gassette & Loyd is reorganized as R. R. Donnelley & Sons . . . Grover Cleveland is elected mayor of Buffalo, then Governor of New York . . . Ibsen's* A Doll's House *is performed in English for the first time, in Milwaukee . . . Thomas Alva Edison designs the first hydroelectric plant, in Appleton, Wisconsin . . . The Knights of Columbus fraternal organization of Catholic men is formed in New Haven, Connecticut.*

II

Reuben H. Donnelley, Entrepreneur

(1886–1917)

Reuben Donnelley was a real entrepreneur in directory publishing. While he sustained his commitment to the future of the telephone directory, he was always spinning out new products, always trying to anticipate people's needs for information and to capitalize on them. In 1890, the printing firm of R. R. Donnelley & Sons was reorganized and incorporated, and Reuben Donnelley formally took on the publication of the Chicago telephone directory. In that year, the directory first appeared with "Reuben H. Donnelley, Publisher" on the title page.[1]

For the thirty years, from 1887, when Reuben became Manager of the Chicago Directory Company, to 1917, when that company was dissolved and the Reuben H. Donnelley Corporation was chartered, the telephone directory remained strictly a Donnelley business, even though it was undoubtedly produced by the staff of the Chicago Directory Company. This fact suggests that Reuben Donnelley was careful to protect his proprietary interest in this venture. In later years, he experimented with a variety of more specialized classified directories, but none appeared to reward his entrepreneurship as well as this original creation.

Publications of the Chicago Directory Company

For the first 20 years of Donnelley's leadership of the Chicago Directory Company, the principal publication continued to be the annual city directory. As the extravagance of the Chicago World's Fair of 1893 clearly showed, Chicago was self-consciously proud of its rapid growth, and the issuing of the annual city directory was a focal point for celebration over continuing expansion. Each year, for about three weeks, the "army of canvassers" would descend on the city, going house-to-house for the names and occupations of residents, and identifying the businesses in all the many office buildings, shops, and factories for the business directory.

As the following notice in a paper of 1903 suggests, the city eagerly awaited Donnelley's calculation of the current population:

> Chicago's new directory is to be issued July 8. Enthusiasts are preparing to continue the Fourth celebrations over to the date named in hope that it will be shown that the city has 2,000,000 population. The Directory man may as well prepare to meet his doom if he shall not figure out everything satisfactorily.[2]

The separate *Lakeside Annual Business Directory* developed at this time into a publication of equal importance in its own field. As an offprint from the city directory, this book was not unique in the basic information it provided, but it contained many special features that made it distinctive and included information not to be found in the city directory, such as an alphabetical list of all the businesses and businessmen in Chicago. Undoubtedly one of its most distinctive features, however, was its appearance. Before Reuben Donnelley took over the management of the directories, the business directory appeared very modestly each year in a cardboard cover with advertising on both front and back. After 1887, it was transformed into "the familiar Red Book," bound in "brilliant red and gilt."[3]

In addition to these established directories, Donnelley developed various new publications to be handled by the Chicago Directory Company. One of these was *The Blue Book*, often called "The Society Blue Book," which first appeared in 1890. Although Donnelley denied that this was intended to be a social register, news releases announcing its appearance each year were typically accompanied by humorous cartoons or poems about the anxiety many people felt over whether or not they would find their names in *The Blue Book*. This directory of about 25,000 "carefully selected" residents included the inhabitants of the city's most fashionable neighborhoods and suburbs, as well as the members of its clubs and philanthropic organizations. In a list of residences by street, it indicated "calling days," and the alphabetical list of individuals gave the addresses of summer residences. *The Blue Book* also included membership lists of clubs and churches. Clearly intended to provide useful information to a carefully targeted subgroup of the city's population, this directory must have provided

---

1886: *The first directories: The Chicago Telephone Directory is published . . . The Statue of Liberty is dedicated in New York Harbor . . . George Westinghouse establishes the Westinghouse Electric Company . . . Robert Louis Stevenson publishes two popular novels,* The Strange Case of Dr. Jekyll and Mr. Hyde, *and* Kidnapped . . . *Apache Chief Geronimo surrenders to General Nelson A. Miles, ending the Apache Indian Wars in the Southwest.*

rich opportunities for the canvassers of the Chicago Directory Company to sell advertising.[4]

One project of this period that did not come to fruition was a listing of automobile dealers and service stations. The prospectus for this directory, sent out in 1904 to potential advertisers, is revealing and highly prophetic. In it Donnelley enunciated a clearly developed concept of directory usage and value. The list, he stated, would be "arranged both alphabetically and by streets and sections of the city—after the manner of our well-known *Blue Book*—to permit the instant location of the nearest agent, repair shop, charging station, etc." Such a list, he argued "should possess unusual advantages as a means for best presenting the claims of an advertiser to that selected section of the public he wishes to reach." Finally, Donnelley pointed out, "automobile owners are people of means," and the directory would be designed to appeal particularly to them: "We shall get out this book, in a modest way, as an EDITION DE LUXE, with gilt-lettered, flexible leather binding, high class paper and typography." Donnelley's concept of this directory foreshadowed the strategy of targeting lucrative market segments and the later development of Donnelley Marketing out of the division that produced a list of automobile owners. Equally significant, however, is his early articulation of the principle that the value of directory advertising to business owners is dependent upon the usefulness of the directory to consumers, a relationship of fundamental importance in the development of the directory industry.[5]

In April of 1905, the Chicago Directory Company brought out another new publication, *The Lakeside Annual Guide to Streets and Avenues of Chicago.* This small book was "one of the most convenient little publications possible," asserted one newspaper, "for the use not only of strangers but of well-informed citizens of Chicago." It contained, in addition to a street directory, lists and descriptions of places of interest and a street map that included both streetcar and elevated rail lines. Although Donnelley had other interests outside the directory business at this time, his entrepreneurism was clearly a strong positive force in the company.[6]

Other Ventures

In 1891, Reuben Donnelley launched *Chicago Securities,* a publication directed toward the business or "financial" men of Chicago. The following review, from the New York paper, *The Financier,* for May 4, 1903, suggests its contents and the prestige it brought to its publisher:

> For twelve years it has been the aim of the publishers to make this work a recognized and indispensable handbook of the financial, industrial, and commercial interests of Chicago, and in its present form [it] is an authority on every question treated. The volume

is bound in strong cloth and contains about 500 pages. Typographically, the work is excellent. General analyses and statistics of the following matters are thoroughly featured: Chicago Exchanges, Membership list of the Stock Exchange, Securities listed, Municipal, county and park bonds, Chicago Clearing house, National and State banks, Trust Companies, Gas and Electric Light Companies, Street and Elevated Railways, Industrials, Miscellaneous Companies, Directory of Directors, Stock and Bond Investment tables, etc. [7]

In addition this "invaluable digest" also typically contained a lengthy introduction that analyzed the financial scene, comparing the development of Chicago to other cities, especially New York. It is not unlikely that Donnelley himself wrote this material, since this was a period of his life when he was very much a part of the financial world of Chicago. [8]

A personal "venture" of this period was Donnelley's marriage to Laura Thorne in 1892. Mrs. Donnelley was part of a prominent Chicago family, the founders of Montgomery Ward, and throughout her married life she was a leader in many of the city's charitable organizations. In 1895, the Donnelleys had a son, Thorne Donnelley, and four years later, a daughter. Eleanor. [9]

In 1895, Donnelley charted new waters for his business career, opening a brokerage firm in partnership with Newell C. Knight, of Evanston, and relinquishing his position as manager of the Chicago Directory Company to his chief compiler, E. J. Dillon. Knight, Donnelley & Company was a very successful brokerage house, and it expanded rapidly. Within two years Donnelley was chosen a member of the Governing Committee of the Chicago Stock Exchange. By 1901, the partnership moved its office to larger quarters in the imposing Rookery Building, and Reuben Donnelley was elected without opposition to be President of the Stock Exchange, a position he filled for three years. [10] In the second half of 1905, however, Knight, Donnelley & Company failed and went out of business, avoiding bankruptcy by paying off its debts at about 28 cents on the dollar. Donnelley returned to the position of Manager of the Chicago Directory Company.

Focus on the Telephone Directory

During the decade of Reuben Donnelley's career as a broker, the

---

1890: *The printing firm of R. R. Donnelley & Sons is reorganized and incorporated . . . The United States population doubles that of the beginning of the Civil War, to 62,979,766 . . . The first Army-Navy football game is played, at West Point (Navy 24, Army 0) . . . Poems by Emily Dickinson is published posthumously . . . Sequoia and Yosemite National Parks are established in California.*

classified telephone directory remained a relatively insignificant publication, much overshadowed by the more widely used city directory. Undoubtedly this was due in part to a decision made in 1889 by the Chicago Telephone Company to prohibit display advertising in the classified list. This dictum was not reversed until 1901. By then, the classified telephone directory had grown to 300 pages, about three times larger than the directory of 1886. But the *Lakeside Annual Business Directory* was three times larger still and had grown at a faster rate. Although the people of Chicago clearly valued the usefulness of a classified business directory, the telephone company was slow to recognize the potential for the same usefulness in its own publication.[11]

At the time, neither businesses nor consumers had come to rely on the telephone as a principal means of communication. In the history of the telephone in America, the period from 1878 to 1886 was one of experimentation, both with equipment and with the various elements necessary to a communication system. In the next decade equipment vastly improved and the basic components of a smooth-running system of national scope were put into place. Still, at the turn of the century, telephones were almost exclusively in the hands of businessmen. In many places, the cost of leasing a phone had risen close to $250 per year, as rates were used to subsidize earlier expensive development.

In 1896, the Bell companies introduced the message rate system, whereby the basic rental cost of a telephone was reduced dramatically and customers were charged at a fixed rate for usage beyond a specified minimum amount. In this way, the cost of a telephone was brought within reach of many householders, and large-scale business users supported the rapid expansion of the system into residential communities around the nation. Use of the telephone then spread rapidly. In the decade between 1886 and 1896, the number of telephones had grown from roughly three to roughly six per 1,000 population nationally. By 1900, that figure had jumped to over 17 per 1,000. Like most cities, Chicago was ahead of the national average, with 20.4 telephones per 1,000 inhabitants. By 1906, the national figure had grown to 57 telephones per 1,000 people.[12]

These statistics held the promise of a substantial reward for Reuben Donnelley's sustained faith in the classified telephone directory, and there is good evidence that he recognized that promise. Beginning in 1906, he aggressively sought telephone directory business outside of Chicago. With his eye on the New York City directory, he made contact with the New York Telephone Company, and he came away in 1906 with contracts for the classified directories of Buffalo, Rochester, Albany, and Troy.[13]

In the fall of 1906, a missed connection gave Donnelley a day to spend in Cincinnati, where he convinced the owner of the Cincinnati and Suburban Telephone Company, Bayard Kilgour, to give him a publishing contract for his company's directory. By Donnelley's own account, Kilgour was a dour gentleman who listened silently for an hour an a half while the eager Chicagoan laid out his concept and vision of directory publishing. Then Kilgour made him tell the entire story again to his assistant. But in the end he accepted Donnelley's contention that he could "improve our directory operation." Reuben Donnelley was one step farther along his way to the establishment of a specialized telephone directory business of national scope.[14]

Shortly after winning the Cincinnati contract, he obtained the business of the Wisconsin Telephone Company for its Milwaukee directory. These two new Donnelley directories made their debut simultaneously, in June of 1907. They were the first to appear in major cities outside of Chicago. Later in the summer of 1907, yet another Donnelley classified directory came out in Providence, Rhode Island. All of these books were printed in Chicago by R. R. Donnelley & Sons, and each of them bore the name "Reuben H. Donnelley, Publisher" on its title page.

The Donnelley Brothers

With these new contracts Reuben Donnelley embarked on the phase of his career that was to lead directly to the creation of the Reuben H. Donnelley Corporation. Since first putting his name on the Chicago Classified Telephone Directory as Publisher in 1890, he had maintained his proprietorship over this business, distinct from all the other directory ventures in which he had been involved. Now he began to develop the telephone directory business, not as an officer of the Chicago Directory Company but as a Vice President of the family printing firm, R. R. Donnelley & Sons, in close partnership with his younger brother, Thomas Elliott

---

1891: Chicago Securities *is launched . . . Stanford White designs Madison Square Garden in New York City . . . The University of Chicago is founded, with an endowment from John D. Rockefeller . . . Physical education professor James Naismith invents basketball in Springfield, Massachusetts . . . Edwin Booth makes his final appearance as an actor, performing in* Hamlet *at the Brooklyn Academy of Music.*

1903: Lakeside Annual Business Directory *is published . . . President Theodore Roosevelt orders warships to Panama to protect "free and uninterrupted transit across the Isthmus" . . . Jack London publishes* Call of the Wild *. . . Frank Lloyd Wright completes the first of his "prairie style" homes, in Illinois . . . An experimental electrical trolley is installed in Scranton, Pennsylvania . . . Picasso paints "La Vie," a work representative of his "Blue Period."*

Donnelley. This strategy was given concrete expression when he moved his personal office away from the Chicago Directory Company into the Donnelley offices in the Lakeside Press Building at Plymouth Place and Polk Street in 1907.

Reuben and "Ted" were very different but highly complementary in their personal characteristics and style, and they were extremely close. Reuben was known for his wit. His family, strongly influenced by its matriarch, Naomi Shenstone Donnelley, took its religious belief and practice very seriously. But within the family circle, Reuben was known to joke that he was the most regular churchgoer because he went every year at Easter. Ted was the quieter and more serious of the two brothers. He was extremely hardworking, an active church man, and a leader in Chicago's Sunday Evening Club. Reuben was a devoted sportsman, who particularly enjoyed hunting wild fowl. Once, after Ted had spent a weekend preparing the figures for a new contract they were working on, he called Reuben's office on Monday morning, only to be reminded that duck hunting season had begun and Reuben would be away from his desk for at least a week.[15]

Ted seems not to have minded Reuben's more easygoing style, however, and was fond of drawing the contrast between himself and his brother. If both of them had had the same experience, Ted would say, he himself might return and describe what had happened. But if they returned and Reuben told the story, he would begin to feel that they had had a real adventure. Clearly Ted was not without a sense of humor, but he greatly admired his witty and charming older brother.[16]

Those who worked with the Donnelley brothers in these years knew them as "T.E." and "R.H." In their collaboration on the Chicago telephone directory, one Donnelley printer remembered, "R. H. determined technical matters, such as, alphabetization, abbreviation, headings, etc. on which he was helped by his chief compiler, E. J. Dillon. T. E. decided times, speeds, burdens and markups, after which Alex Loyd did the contact with the Telephone Company. . . . Through it all T. E. Donnelley kept in touch with most details, an interest he maintained as long as he was active in business."[17]

As a Vice President of R. R. Donnelley & Sons, Reuben Donnelley was most active in the sales division. He contributed much to the family business in this capacity, bringing to it the entrepreneurial energy and the fine appreciation of the booming Chicago marketplace that characterized all of his previous business activity. "I was talking the matter over with T. E. yesterday," he wrote in 1910 to a Donnelley salesman out in the field, in Pittsburgh, and

> we are both of the opinion that we are overlooking lots of good
> business in Chicago, which by the way, is the best field in the

country, which you could take care of. . . . Both T. E. and I are
convinced that Chicago has got all the rest of the cities in the
country pushed off the map and that there is more real business
right here than in any other place.[18]

At the same time, a good portion of what Reuben Donnelley
then sold for R. R. Donnelley & Sons was the printing of telephone directories that he himself took on as publisher. The expansion of this business
required that he carry into other cities the distinctive "Chicago-style"
directory that was evolving under the partnership with his brother. The
Donnelleys' long experience both in printing and in publishing Chicago's
city and telephone directories gave them a solid reputation on which to
build this line of business in other cities. In his dual capacity as directory
publisher and as a vice president of the printing firm, Reuben Donnelley
was in the perfect position to push forward with this expansion. Throughout
the decade prior to World War I, he personally either conducted or supervised
all the Donnelley negotiations for telephone directory work, alphabetical
as well as classified, printing as well as publishing.[19]

In Chicago, the Donnelleys' principal contact in the telephone
company was A. Milne Ramsey, who was then making his reputation in
telephone circles as "the dean of directory superintendents." It had been
Ramsey who had allowed the return of display advertising to the Chicago
classified in 1901, and, from then until 1904, he experimented with publishing the classified as a separate book. In 1906, he encouraged R. R.
Donnelley & Sons to adopt an improved type style (later known as "Bell
Gothic") for the alphabetical list. In 1908, on the basis of statistics compiled
by AT&T on the probable growth of telephone usage, he pushed for the
introduction of condensed type, so that more columns could be printed
on every page and the size of the book could be held down as the list of
telephone subscribers grew.[20]

Directory work fitted the capabilities of R. R. Donnelley & Sons
well, because the directories could be printed on presses that had been
installed to handle the Montgomery Ward catalogs. In 1907, R. R. Donnelley
& Sons lost the Ward business that it had held for over a decade, which
provided an added incentive to press forward with a program of expanding
in the directory field. As the Chicago telephone directory grew, it benefited
from the fact that the Ward catalog presses were designed to handle paper
lighter than what was typically used in directories. In addition, because
they printed with the grain of the paper along, rather than across, the
binding edge, they produced more durably bound books. The recombination
of the alphabetical and the classified lists in 1905 made the Chicago telephone
directory large enough to be perfect bound, and this too made it stronger.
Subsequent contracts for books in other cities sometimes specified that the

directory be perfect bound, with "the so-called Donnelley patent binding."

R. R. Donnelley & Sons' chief competitor in directory printing at this time was the Jersey City Printing Company that handled the books for the New York City area, but Jersey City did not produce as well-made a book as did Donnelley. "The result of all this," writes H. P. Zimmerman (Donnelley's chief sales manager in this period), "was that our telephone directories were at least as good and generally considered better than those made elsewhere and this fact did not escape the notice of telephone company managements in other cities." This was the "Chicago-style" of directory that Ramsey and the Donnelleys had developed, and it was this product that Reuben Donnelley sold in upstate New York, Cincinnati, Milwaukee, and Providence.[21]

A New York Office

Yet what Donnelley had to offer also included a more intangible aspect, the sales capability to develop the classified directory into an advertising medium that could compete with the business section of the city directory. Certainly this was an important part of the product that he took to New York City in 1909. The classified telephone directory for Manhattan had been printed since 1901 by the Jersey City Printing Company and published by the Alcolm Company, which was partly owned by the owners of Jersey City. It was called *The Alcolm Red Book.* Reuben Donnelley purchased the rights to this directory and took over much of its staff. But the *Manhattan Red Book* that he produced for the first time in July of 1909 was very different from the old Alcolm product. The contrast between them is clearly stated in the reminiscence of one Alcolm employee who joined Reuben Donnelley in 1909. The Alcolm directory, he noted,

---

1905: *The Chicago Directory Company publishes* The Street Directory . . . *The Rotary Club is founded in Chicago by Paul Harris, a lawyer . . . President Theodore Roosevelt initiates the peace conference at Portsmouth, New Hampshire, that ends the Russo-Japanese War and for which he will receive the Nobel Peace Prize in 1906 . . . George Bernard Shaw's* Mrs. Warren's Profession *is closed by police in New York City after one performance, at the behest of Anthony Comstock of the Society for the Prevention of Vice.*

1907: *New Donnelley directories appear in Cincinnati, Milwaukee and Providence . . . Oklahoma becomes the 46th State . . . The U. S. Navy "Great White Fleet" sails around the world . . . George W. Goethals is chosen to direct construction of the Panama Canal . . . The Lusitania, the largest steamship in the world, sails from Liverpool to New York on its maiden voyage.*

was very poorly compiled and so full of typographical errors that the Telephone Company was very glad when Reuben Donnelley took it over. In contrast with the Chicago Classified Telephone Directory it was also very poorly sold. Special headings and bold face listings were the only forms of advertising—no space items, no informationals, etc. . . . . The advertising sales on an issue basis did not exceed $10,000 and, for instance, the whole borough of Bronx only yielded $300.00. . . . After the first issue of the book was out, Mr. Donnelley transferred one of the Chicago salesmen to New York both to sell and to teach the other salesmen how it should be done.[22]

By 1910, the *Manhattan Red Book*, printed on yellow paper with a red cover, was patterned on the Chicago style of classified directories. The merger of two companies, New York Bell Telephone and New York and New Jersey Telephone, brought Manhattan, Brooklyn, Queens, Long Island, and several major upstate New York cities under a single company, New York Telephone. Following this reorganization, Reuben Donnelley acquired contracts to publish directories for Brooklyn and Queens. He established an office on Fulton Street, near the offices of AT&T and Western Electric at 195 Broadway, and he established a reputation for himself as a leader in the directory business.

Donnelley cultivated and maintained good relationships with telephone company management and was especially close to the men in Western Electric who were pushing hard to establish their own company as purchasing agent for the Bell System for items such as directories. At the same time, he had a friendly relationship with his major rival, Albert Von Hoffmann. The Donnelley's were investors in Von Hoffmann's National Directory Company, and they printed his St. Louis directory, though he

---

1909: *The New York Office . . .* The Manhattan Red Book *appears in July . . . The Queensboro Bridge is opened in March, and the Manhattan Bridge in December, both spanning the East River . . . William Howard Taft is inaugurated as 27th President, and soon sets aside 3 million acres of public lands in the west for conservation purposes . . . Incandescent lamps replace carbide flame jets as automobile headlights.*

1915: The Chicago Red Book . . . *Alexander Graham Bell in New York City calls Dr. Thomas A. Watson in San Francisco . . . The United States Coast Guard is created by Congress . . . D.W. Griffith's* The Birth of a Nation *has its first showing, in Los Angeles . . . The British liner Lusitania is sunk by a German torpedo ten miles off the Irish coast . . . The first transatlantic radiotelephone communication is sent between Arlington, Virginia, and the Eiffel Tower in Paris.*

had barely beaten Reuben Donnelley to this piece of publishing business in 1907.[23]

In the years leading up to World War I, Reuben Donnelley's directory business continued to expand geographically, though not as fast as before. He took on the directories for Wisconsin in 1913 and won new contracts with Illinois Bell in 1914 for directories outside of Chicago. Of greater import for the future direction of the enterprise, however, was a tremendous increase in the scope of his existing business. In 1909, he began to publish "neighborhood" directories for the Austin, Rodgers Park, and South Shore sections of Chicago. Then his Manhattan business was augmented by separate directories for Brooklyn and Queens. Moreover, the big city directories themselves grew at such a rapid rate that handling them became a job of much greater proportions than it had been just a few years earlier. Between 1909 and 1916 the size of the Manhattan classified almost doubled, while its circulation tripled. The Chicago directory kept pace, and, by 1915, it was large enough to be separated, permanently this time, from the alphabetical.

Donnelley gave this new publication a new name, *The Chicago Red Book.* His use of this title celebrated his expansion into New York, where he had taken over both the *Alcolm Red Book* and the *Brooklyn Red Book.* At the same time, it symbolized his own long association with directory publishing in Chicago, echoing the name, "the familiar Red Book," that he had coined for the Chicago business directory some 20-odd years before.

III

The Reuben H. Donnelley Corporation
(1917–1929)

After almost three decades, the business of Reuben H. Donnelley, Publisher, had clearly outgrown the rather loose institutional framework in which it had flourished. The publications that had originally been the mainstay of the Chicago Directory Company, the city and business directories and *The Blue Book*, had dwindled in importance by this time, though the Directory Delivery Department was still busy. In 1914, a list department was created to handle a new line of business—the selling of directory lists to advertisers as the basis for mailings. With the nontelephone directories on the wane and direct mail still in its infancy, the Chicago Directory Company increasingly became an adjunct to Donnelley's telephone directory business. At the same time, the Directory Division of the printing firm, R. R. Donnelley & Sons, was increasingly independent and self-directed, standing firmly on its own well-earned reputation in this field. All along, it had printed directories for Reuben Donnelley's competitors, and, in 1913, for the first time, it negotiated a substantial directory contract outside of Chicago without the intervention of "R. H."[1]

Early in 1917, Donnelley embarked on a new project, *National Classified Telephone Directory of the United States.* Between January and September, he established offices in 14 cities around the country and hired close to 100 salesmen to sell listings and advertisements in this directory, which he proposed to distribute twice a year, free of charge to 100,000 purchasing agents, public agencies, and libraries. His expenses during this organization period were tremendous, about 11 percent of his total assets, and the management of this new undertaking, in addition to the rest of his directory business, clearly called for a new corporate structure.

The Reuben H. Donnelley Corporation was officially chartered in New York state on September 4, 1917. Its principal office was 227 Fulton Street in New York City, with a "branch" at 633 Plymouth Court in Chicago, where most of the corporate business was done at special meetings of the directors. At the first directors' meeting on September 18, 1917, Reuben

Donnelley gave the corporation life by signing over to it his personal business assets, roughly a quarter of a million dollars' worth of directory business.[2]

As the principal owner of the Chicago Directory Company, Donnelley included among these assets the Chicago city and business directories, the other publications of the firm having been discontinued prior to this time. Now he allowed these two directories to die out as well, although the Chicago Directory Company itself was never officially dissolved. In practice, the lines between it and the business of Reuben H. Donnelley, Publisher, had always been blurred. Donnelley had carefully maintained the official distinction between the publications of the two, but from 1886 onward the staff of the Chicago Directory Company had worked on all of the Donnelley directories. Now they were simply absorbed into the new Reuben H. Donnelley Corporation.[3]

The grand venture that had inaugurated the start of the new corporation, *The National Classified Telephone Directory,* soon foundered on the economic upheaval of World War I and the inflation of paper and printing costs that immediately followed it. In December of 1919, the board of directors, noting falling profit margins, voted to curtail this operation sharply, publishing a smaller directory once instead of twice annually, with only eight sales offices instead of 14.[4] But the entrepreneurial initiative that had brought this publication into being had already given life to another new directory venture—*Donnelley's Industrial Directory* for the "Great Chicago Market," encompassing Michigan, Wisconsin, Iowa, Indiana, and Illinois. Aimed at the same class of users as the national directory, this book was confined in geographical scope to the region that Donnelley knew best and had always relied upon for the financial base of his operations. He had not given up on his vision of a national classified telephone directory but had retreated temporarily to familiar territory. As if to finalize this drawing back to the Chicago base, the corporation was rechartered in Illinois in January, 1920.[5]

Directory Services and New Titles

Reuben Donnelley's business advanced steadily from this foundation during the 1920's, its expansion following three main lines: elaboration of his existing directory business, experimentation with publishing new directories, and development of the direct mail business. In 1920, the first Chicago Suburban telephone directory was published, opening up a rich new field for Donnelley salesmen. New directory contracts were obtained from Illinois Bell for books in Illinois and Indiana, along with a contract to sell boldface listings into the Chicago alphabetical directory. Donnelley also developed a Buyers' Service Bureau in the Chicago office, which he viewed as an important complement to the directory business. The Red

Book Information Bureau, as it was first called, handled telephone requests for information on where to locate products or services not covered in the classified directory. The information that Donnelley gathered in this way helped directory advertising salesmen to develop new headings. At the same time, it was a significant benefit to directory users and advertisers, and it was promoted by the corporation as an important part of "the Donnelley principle of Directory Service."[6]

Another area of expansion at this time was the delivery business, originally called the "Distribution Department." Donnelley had operated a New York office that handled delivery of his classified directories since 1909, and the Chicago Directory Company staff had performed this operation as well. In 1920, however, a distinct Delivery Division of the Reuben H. Donnelley Corporation began to take shape, with the purchase of the National Delivery Service Company of Philadelphia. Donnelley continued to operate this business as purchased, including warehousing and window display installation as well as delivery, direct mail, and merchandising.

At the same time, Donnelley was pushing ahead with new directory ventures. In 1921, he launched a nationwide project, *The Manufacturers and Distributors Directories.* These so-called "Industrial Directories" or "M & D" directories were modeled on the original industrial directory for the "Great Chicago Market," but they were published and sold locally in nine different regions of the country. Within a few years the regions were reduced to only two, the Central District and the Eastern District, but this venture was fundamentally successful and continued to be sound financially throughout Donnelley's lifetime. Less successful, more specialized directory ventures in these years were *The Bride's Book* and *The National Jewelry Catalog.*

Direct Mail

A third line of business that Donnelley developed in this period was direct mail marketing. This was a natural outgrowth of the directory business in the sense that both were dependent on the compilation of a

---

1917: The National Classified Telephone Directory of the United States, *with offices in fourteen cities, is launched; The Reuben H. Donnelley Corporation is officially chartered in New York State . . . President Wilson severs diplomatic relations with Germany when the U.S. liner Housatonic is sunk by a German submarine . . . George M. Cohan writes the World War I song, "Over There" . . . The first baseball game played in New York City's Polo Grounds leads to the arrest of managers John McGraw, Giants, and Christy Mathewson, Cincinnati Reds, for the Blue Law violation of playing on Sunday.*

list of names and addresses. Beyond this, however, they differed considerably. Direct Mail was both more aggressive and more tightly focused on a few selected products. In addition, it quickly moved beyond the very general list of city residents that could be derived from the directories to more selective lists, intended to yield a higher percentage of likely buyers for the products being marketed by mail. Reuben Donnelley's scheme for an automobile owners' directory in 1904 shows that he recognized early the advertising potential of such selectivity, and lists of automobile owners provided the backbone of the Direct Mail Division as it developed out of the Chicago Directory Company's List Department after 1914.[7]

In 1921, Direct Mail expanded greatly, opening an office in New York and later acquiring the Moreland Advertising Company. B. E. Moreland joined Donnelley in what was then called the Mailing Service Department, as Director of Special Campaigns. He brought with him his experience in marketing, his staff and physical plant, and his "patented specialties, the 'Daily Dime Saver' and the 'Moreland Self-Envelope Illustrated Letter' . . . an attractive addition to our regular Mail Advertising line."[8]

The year 1922 brought another important acquisition for the Direct Mail Division, the M & F Mailing System of Nevada, Iowa. Reuben Donnelley went to Nevada to investigate this company, which began as a one-man compilation department in 1919 and had grown to an operation sending out 30 million pieces of mail a year. What Donnelley also found in Nevada were two young men whom he sincerely wanted to recruit into his corporation—David L. Harrington and A. M. Anderson. "We received a very pleasant letter from Mr. D. L. Harrington," noted the Lakeside Press Magazine in May, 1922. "He enclosed a copy of the 'M & F News,' which clearly indicates that our 'adopted son' in Iowa is going to be a very welcome member of the Donnelley family." This prophecy proved true both in the short and the long run.[9]

Direct Mail was a dynamic part of the corporation for the rest of Donnelley's active leadership. In 1923, the division acquired the Efficiency Mail List Company of New York City, a concern that compiled lists of auto owners and developed statistics that made the lists more useful. This operation

---

1921: *The* Manufacturers and Distributors Directories *launched; the Direct Mail Division expands significantly. . . DeWitt Wallace founds* Reader's Digest *. . . President Warren G. Harding proclaims November 11 Armistice Day, a national holiday . . . The Jack Dempsey-George Carpentier fight in Jersey City is won by Dempsey in a fourth round knockout . . . Station WJZ in Newark, New Jersey, broadcasts the first play-by-play description of the World Series between the New York teams, the National League Giants and the American League Yankees.*

was moved to Nevada, where its manager became head of a statistical department.[10] In 1925, Direct Mail expanded again with the creation of an office in Los Angeles, California.

A Respected Leader

The decade during which Reuben Donnelley presided over the corporation he had created was one of significant growth. It was also a time when the organization rode high on the crest of Donnelley's personal success and prestige. A prominent Chicagoan since the turn of the century, when he had served as president of the Chicago Stock Exchange, Donnelley was a well-known philanthropist in the city. During World War I he had served as a food administrator for Lake County, and both he and his wife were officers of the Red Cross. He was a charter member of the Better Business Bureau and had been active in the creation of the Association of American Directory Publishers, an organization devoted primarily to combating fraudulent directory operations that collected advertising revenues for nonexistent publications. In his fifties, Reuben Donnelley attained a wide reputation as a leader in the advertising industry and, in particular, as an energetic advocate of "truth in advertising."[11]

In 1920, Donnelley served a brief term, from March to June, as president of the Associated Advertising Clubs of the World. In this position he traveled around the Midwest and as far as California, speaking on the significance and the utility of advertising in American society. For many years, he had been an extremely active leader behind the scenes in this organization. But since the death of his wife, Laura, in the influenza epidemic of 1918, Donnelley's health had begun to fail, and he declined to stay on in the presidency. "There is universal regret that Mr. Donnelley refuses absolutely to consider a renomination as president," reported The Fourth Estate from the Associated Clubs' convention in June, 1920. "Mr. Donnelley has clearly shown at every meeting over which he has presided that he is a natural leader: besides being serious and level headed, he has a fund of humor which catches the crowd."

Reuben Donnelley's strength of character and warmth of personality were appreciated within his own organization as well. Sometime around the turn of the century, he instituted the policy of giving every employee a turkey at Christmas, and after a successful hunting trip he was likely to leave a barrel of ducks by the office entrance for people to help themselves. In others ways as well, he was careful to make employees feel that their contributions to the success of the firm were appreciated. Without the "hearty support and effective team work" of everyone, he asserted in his Christmas message of 1922, "the 'Old Man' and the so-called heads could have accomplished nothing." In 1924, as a tangible recognition of service, he inaugurated a Twenty-Five Year club with a dinner at the Black-stone Hotel and the awarding of commemorative pins. [12]

The two Donnelley companies remained very close during this period, sharing employee benefit organizations, a company publication, *The Lakeside Press Magazine,* and activities such as company picnics, golf and tennis tournaments, and bowling leagues. This was in large part because the Donnelley brothers were themselves so compatible. Every day they would meet at their reserved corner table in the restaurant of Dearborn Station, "T. E." coming over from Plymouth Court and "R. H.," after 1925, from his new offices at 320 East 22nd Street. Each spring, at the combined company picnic, "T. E." would be the first batter up for the R. R. Donnelley team and "R. H." for the Reuben H. Donnelley Corporation. With a larger pool of employees to draw from, the printers were the stronger baseball team—until the year that Reuben Donnelley hired a semi-pro ball club to deliver the Chicago Classified. In that year, R. R. Donnelley & Sons bowed out before the end of the second inning. [13]

The Directory Business in the 1920s

In the 1920s, directory advertising, like all business and, indeed, like American society in general, was a high-spirited, "rough-and-tumble" affair, and Reuben Donnelley moved comfortably within it. In his New York offices, he was "a master in the art" of entertaining telephone company executives in the style that they appreciated. Typically, the Donnelley brothers would ride to New York on either the "Broadway," Reuben's favorite train, or the "Century," which Ted preferred—arguing amicably about the superiority of one over the other. Arriving on Tuesday morning, they would try to complete their business in time, if Reuben had his way, to attend the Ziegfeld Follies on Wednesday afternoon. Then they would catch the other train back to Chicago. Occasionally, during Prohibition, Reuben was entertained by the eccentric Albert Von Hoffmann, head of the rival National Directory Company, at his camp in the Ozarks. There Von Hoffmann operated a fish hatchery, so his guests would be sure to catch a fish, and a school for brewing and distilling, so that if "anyone accused him of having whiskey or beer on the place he would say, 'Of course—you can't teach distilling or brewing without making the product.' "[14]

There was a also good bit of the "rough-and-tumble" spirit in Donnelley's offices. The men who were "the bosses" at 22nd Street often kept illicit bottles in their desks, and cuspidors nearby. While there was some training for new salesmen, it was generally believed that "the actual street experience is, in the final analysis, the real directory school." But the streets of Chicago and New York could be very tough places in which to do business then. One suspects that a number of the men who rose to the top in directory sales in this period did so by cultivating a flamboyant style, like the Chicago salesman who had been sent to New York to teach the former Alcolm men how to sell ads in the *Red Book*. "This salesman told me," Abe Epstein later remembered,

> that he wanted me to go with him to learn how a decent size sale could be made. We took a street car up to the Bronx and about a block away from the customer, got into a taxi cab. We drove up to the door of the Colonial Carpet Cleaning Company and the salesman told the taxi driver to keep the flag down and the meter running. We then asked for the president of the company and the salesman said he had come all the way from Chicago to find out why the biggest carpet cleaning company in New York didn't have the biggest ad in the book, and promptly sold him a $600 ad.[15]

In general, the hiring and training of this period was done by the sales managers on a small scale, although there was an "M & D Sales School" in Chicago for men hired to sell ads in the industrial directories in the various district offices. Managers screening applicants for the job of Donnelley salesman were advised to look for "certain fundamental qualities":

> The first impression of physical fitness and the very necessary clean cut appearance are factors; determination to get the job counts; honesty of purpose; mental fitness and flexibility is of vital importance; sales poise; confidence in their ability to handle the job; men who talk well—not with too much emphasis or vocabulary but rather those whose eyes and words co-ordinate convincingly—in brief, men who can sell me on the idea that they can properly represent our house and its traditions.

Once hired, these men would be given a few of the highlights on general publicity; . . . the 'directory publisher's answer' to some of the more general objections encountered; . . . [and an understanding of] the importance of a knowledge of directory classifications and headings." It might be suggested that they should be prepared to present ideas for advertising copy and that they should be able to show to a prospect advertisements by competitors in his line of business. For the most part, however,

---

1922–1925: *The* Direct Mail Division *expands dramatically, with new acquisitions in Iowa, New York City and Los Angeles . . . In 1925, Nellie Tayloe Ross becomes the first woman governor in the United States, in Wyoming . . . F. Scott Fitzgerald publishes* The Great Gatsby, *and Ernest Hemingway* Our Time *. . . Tennessee schoolteacher John T. Scopes is arrested for teaching the theory of evolution, and is convicted at the "Monkey Trial."*

salesmen had to learn by doing, and, like Abe Epstein, by observing those who were more experienced.[16]

Reuben Donnelley was aloof from this aspect of the business. His expertise was that of a publisher, recognizing people's need for a specific kind of information and shaping a publication to fill that need. Of course, he understood the advertising value of his directories. But if the function of the book was understood, Donnelley believed, it would sell itself. In fact, he was wary of too highly developed selling skills and cautioned new salesmen against manipulating potential advertisers. To one incoming group, he asserted that it was the salesman's "responsibility to bring in all possible legitimate business." Still, he cautioned them: "Sell to the big companies all the advertising they will buy—and more; but avoid the overselling of small companies who might be induced in a moment of enthusiasm to take more advertising in one medium than they can profitably carry."[17]

Donnelley's Legacy

After January 1927, Reuben Donnelley was not an active force in the corporation. He spent much of the last two years of his life in the hospital or confined to his suite of rooms at the Blackstone Hotel. The influence of his reputation was still great among his employees, however, and it reached a new peak in December 1927, when he sought out, and repaid with interest all of the investors who had lost money when Knight, Donnelley & Company had gone out of business in 1905. This was a crowning achievement for a career in which a fortune had been lost and regained and which had been largely devoted, in its final decade, to the promotion of honesty and integrity in business.

He died on February 25, 1929. Seven months later, "Black Friday" on the New York Stock Exchange would set in motion forces that would alter forever fundamental aspects of American business life. In adjusting to these changes, his successors at the head of the Reuben H. Donnelley Corporation would shift the emphasis in the directory business, transforming it from what was primarily a publishing firm into a full-fledged sales organization.

Donnelley's entrepreneurial drive made his company the largest independent sales-agent for Bell System directories. In the first decades of

---

1929: *Reuben H. Donnelley dies on February 25th, and George W. Overton succeeds him as President . . . The Academy Awards are presented for the first time . . . The stock market crashes over four days in late October . . . President Hoover signs an income tax reduction bill . . . Hoagy Carmichael writes the song "Star Dust," and the radio show "Amos and Andy" has its national premiere.*

the twentieth century, when many telephone companies competed for predominance, he had cast his lot with the ultimate winner and had succeeded in capturing a healthy share of the high-growth market of his era. The passage of the Graham Act in 1921 ended competition in the telephone industry. Declaring monopolies appropriate in this vital utility, Congress forced each community to choose a single telephone company, and AT&T emerged with close to 90 percent of the business, relegating the remaining independent telephone companies to the more isolated, thinly populated areas of the county. Except for the business of these independents, the act effectively closed off competition in the directory industry as well.

The contracts with Bell companies in New York and Illinois gave Donnelley security within its directory regions, and, in the 1930s and 1940s, the company won more Bell business, creating two new regions in the Northeast, encompassing Pennsylvania, Delaware, Maryland, Virginia, West Virginia, and the District of Columbia. However, Reuben Donnelley's death coincided with the beginning of a shift in population that made the West and South the high-growth areas of the mid-20th century. Firmly established as the largest independent directory organization within the Bell System, the company was, in effect, constrained by its own success from expanding into these regions. The 1949 contract that created Donnelley's Chesapeake & Potomac Region was its last new piece of Bell business. Thus, as the orientation of AT&T shifted in the monopoly period from competition to public service, the focus in Donnelley would also shift from expansion to preservation of its established position. The entrepreneurial spirit that had created the company would have to be set aside until competition was once again introduced into the telephone and telephone directory industries.

Yet Donnelley's idealism and the standards that he established for "the Donnelley principle of Directory Service" would also prove to be an enduring legacy to his company. And, perhaps, his most valuable gift was in the original act of creating the business—in effecting the marriage of an established advertising medium, the classified directory, with an instrument of the future, the telephone. "The telephone is the door to the, merchant's establishment," Donnelley had instructed Milwaukee businessmen in 1907. "Your advertisement in this directory will reach more people for less money than ANY OTHER advertising medium," he told others in Baraboo, Wisconsin, in 1913.[18] By the time of his death he had been an investor in this concept for more than 40 years.

During his lifetime, the telephone industry passed from its infancy no further than into its childhood. Checked only slightly in its spread during the Depression, the telephone system would expand so rapidly in the years after World War II that, by 1959, "the door" had been opened to 75 percent of all American households, by 1970 to 90 percent. Donnelley's genius as a publisher had been to capture the power of this rising communications industry in print. The future of the Reuben H. Donnelley Corporation as a sales organization lay in the increasing professionalism with which it showed businessmen how to use it.

IV
Through The Depression and World War II
(1930–1950)

The Great Depression hurt the classified directory business in several ways. In most places directory advertising was still a new, unproven medium, and hard times naturally reduced the ability and willingness of business people to spend money on any kind of advertising. As more and more businesses failed, competition for customers, and, with it, the need for advertising, were diminished. Finally, the system of communication that was the lifeline of the directory industry retracted as the economic crisis deepened. Following the national pattern, the percentage of households with telephones dropped from a 1929 high of 42 percent to a low point of 31 percent in 1933. After this, it rose slowly, not regaining 42 percent until 1942. Under these circumstances, directory salesmen often found it difficult to convince their customers of the utility and value of classified advertising.[1]

All of these factors weighed on the Reuben H. Donnelley Corporation, as they did on others in the directory business. The remaining *Manufacturers and Distributors Directories* were discontinued and their sales staff absorbed into the Chicago sales force. The Springfield, Illinois, office was also closed, and the entire downstate Illinois operation fell to a single individual. Corporate profits dropped to $4,660 in 1933, from a high of almost $200,000 two years before.

Yet the directory industry as a whole, and Donnelley along with it, suffered less from the Depression than most businesses. From 1929 to 1933, industry-wide revenues dropped by only 28.5 percent, as compared to a 48.4 percent decline in the value of retail sales nationwide. Moreover, while there were some very bad years, such as 1933, sales peformance was erratic rather than consistently bad, and a strong upward trend was clearly established by 1935. Directory industry revenues reached 1929 levels by 1937, three years before those of general retail sales.[2]

The explanation for this strength and resiliency in the directory industry lies in large measure in the basic fact that, regardless of economic conditions, classified directory advertising remained both valuable and cost-effective. At the same time, Donnelley, along with others in the industry, took steps to improve the effectiveness of directory salesmen, so that they were better able to convey this message to potential advertisers. In 1929, George W. Overton became president of the company. Overton had joined the Chicago Directory Company in 1916 and had been appointed Secretary and Treasurer of the Reuben H. Donnelley Corporation at its establishment in 1917, rising to Vice President by 1928. On becoming President, he began at once to raise the standards for hiring and promotion in the directory division. Within two years the company was well along in a program to provide its salesmen both better training and better support in the field.

A Professional Approach

The first important innovation was the creation of a reference book, *Headings and Related Headings for Classified Telephone Directories,* produced by the Chicago office in 1932. Some eight years earlier, AT&T had established a Directory Department for the purpose of setting standards and developing general policies for the directories of the Bell System. Conferences of Bell company directory managers held in 1924 and 1928 established certain basic principles regarding headings. They decided that every business telephone subscriber should be entitled to one free listing under a broadly descriptive main heading and could also purchase further listings under commodity subheadings that indicated particular products or services. In addition, subscribers could purchase so-called "brand-name representation," which allowed them to display the trade mark of a national company whose products the advertiser handled.[3]

This system created a complex profusion of headings. In fact, there was an almost infinite variety of listings that could be sold, because no restriction was placed on the number of subheadings. For example, under "Book Business" there could be dozens of subheadings such as "Appointment Books," "Art Books," "Astrological Books," "Masonic Books," or "Medical Books." An early attempt to help salesmen deal with the problems

---

1931: *Raymond W. Gunnison establishes the* Trade Papers Division, *restoring publishing as part of the Donnelley operation . . . The Chrysler Building and the Empire State Building are completed in New York City . . . The New York State Legislature begins investigation of Mayor James (Jimmy) Walker of New York City . . . In September, 305 banks close; in October, 522 . . . The Star Spangled Banner is officially designated the United States National Anthem.*

presented by this complicated heading structure was made in 1930, when Donnelley's New York Sales Service Department inaugurated a system of cards, called "Free Listing Leads," that gave the names of businesses under various free, main headings and suggested related headings under which additional listings might be sold. "This system ought to be a knockout," announced *The Lakeside Press Magazine,* and, undoubtedly, it was a big help. But it was only possible to provide cards for half the prospects in the directory, and these encompassed only about half the main headings. Moreover, while in 1930 there were around 2,400 headings in use, just a few years later there were 12,000. A standardized reference work was the only solution. In 1936, Donnelley established a permanent directory heading department to continue updating and refining the all-important heading structure. [4]

The first basic listing of headings, subheadings, and cross-references in a convenient, pocket-sized book, Donnelley's *Headings and Related Headings* was an invaluable reference source. It also represented an advance in sales training. Its introduction described in detail how the information could be used by salesmen to prepare for interviews with prospective advertisers. Figuring out what headings to propose for a particular business was in itself a valuable exercise, because it required finding out about the nature of the business. The publication of this book was the first step toward establishing "pre-planning" as an integral part of Donnelley salesmanship, and it laid the foundation for the training materials and program that were soon to follow.

Clarence Lillyblade and The Donnelley Manual

A central figure in the shaping of company directory policy in these years was Clarence O. Lillyblade, who was General Sales Manager and, after 1935, Vice President in charge of the Illinois/Cincinnati Region. Lillyblade stood out as the consummate advertising man. Impressively tall and handsome, with a sharp, waxed mustache, he was flamboyant, both in dress and behavior. Few people were allowed to see beyond this flashy exterior. Yet beneath it, Lillyblade was serious-minded and absolutely devoted to his profession. In particular, he prided himself on his ability to "separate the important from the unimportant," and in the areas that he deemed important he made contributions of lasting value. [5]

It was Clarence Lillyblade who took the lead in developing sales training at Donnelley in the 1930s. When he took over the Chicago office in 1932, training for new men consisted of two weeks' classes on compilation, contracts, and headings, and for sales technique, no more than one day's observation of a more experienced person at work. District managers held

sales meetings every week, on Saturdays, but these were primarily for comparing notes and assessing the week's results. Lillyblade broke this pattern,
starting off his tenure with a two-day meeting of all the region's salesmen,
in which he gave a demonstration of sales technique—a performance he
was to give at the opening of every canvass and for which he was to become
quite well-known.[6]

   After this, the Saturday meetings were moved into schoolrooms,
complete with students' desks, and they became regular training sessions
for Donnelley salesmen. In November 1932, the Directory Department of
AT&T produced a *Directory Advertising Sales Training Manual* that was made
available to Donnelley for its training program. Most of this manual was
devoted to describing the Bell System and its policies, but it was also a
teaching guide for instructors on selling classified directory advertising.
As such it gives some insight into these early training classes. For example,
in one class students were assigned several businesses from the town of
Ardmore, Oklahoma, for which they were given prospect cards. Using
census data on the city as well as information from a usage survey of 41
Ardmore residences, they were to prepare for premise calls. The manual
indicates that the class as a whole was to go over basic procedures and
etiquette, and that the teacher would present material covering the most
frequently offered objections to directory advertising and how to answer
them. But roles were also prescribed, sometimes with the teacher as the
"customer," and sometimes with students playing both salesman and business-
owner.[7]

   In 1934, Donnelley produced the first of its own training guides,
The Donnelley Manual of Directory Salesmanship. This was less a training
manual than a self-help book. It was published in a red leatherette binding,
and a numbered copy was given to each salesman. Commissioned by Clarence
Lillyblade, it was produced by Trade Ways and based on that firm's obser-
vations of Donnelley salesmen in the field. Lillyblade edited the text and
wrote an introduction, and *The Donnelly Manual* clearly reflects his forceful
style and selling skills. This manual, Lillyblade states in the Foreword,

> is built on practical experience alone and does not contain arm-
> chair theory or guess work. . . . [It] contains concrete information
> that will help *you* take each step that makes for more sales and
> better sales. . . . Your earnest study of this Manual will stimulate
> *real thinking* about directory sales and about how they should be
> made. *The more you think, the more successful you will be.*

The manual opens with two dialogues between salesmen and
customers—one successful and one not—and it continues on through nine
chapters, illustrating each major step in the sales process with more examples
of dialogue. With this approach, *The Donnelley Manual* had the effect of

making each salesman feel as though he were reading his own words. It was something a salesman could turn to after losing a sale to find a suggestion of how he might improve his performance another time. Under "Handling Questions and Objections," for example, he might review the dialogue illustrating "Don't Argue" or "Handling the Obvious Stall." Or, under "Closing the Hard Sale," he could turn to "Four Closing Methods That Work," "Using a Change of Pace", or "Using 'Proof Materials' Effectively." Finally, he could evaluate his overall sales technique more broadly by reviewing the "Self-Analysis" section for each chapter, where he could respond "Yes," "Neutral," or "No" to queries such as, "Do I state my questions directly and without excuse or apology?" "Do I emphasize needs and results throughout my statement of the recommendation?" and "Do I maintain an attitude of helpfulness to the prospect?"[8]

The Donnelley Manual marks a watershed in the company's progress in that it clearly defines directory salesmanship as a profession with specific skills and requirements for success. It came at a time when Donnelley was also beginning to develop a more professionalized system of support on which its salesmen could depend. In the earliest days, Abe Epstein noted, salesmen were given "renewal slips, contract blanks, rate cards, but no PL's, no promotion material, no artwork, no Telephone Company advertising. It was just a door-to-door canvass." By 1932, however, sales support staff were operating in every region, user surveys had been made, and AT&T had been selling its National Trade Mark Service in an organized way for four years. The Manhattan Classified became a million-dollar book with a 14 percent sales gain in 1932, and Abe Epstein was one of the salesmen rewarded for this achievement with a trip to Bermuda.[9]

In 1936, the company introduced the first full-fledged sales aids. Once again, the new materials were primarily the creation of Clarence Lillyblade. "The Road to the Invisible Market" is a striking visual presentation of the concept of the impulsive "need-to-know" motivation for using a directory, when a sudden requirement for goods or services in the home or workplace prompts a person to look for buying information. Its message is transmitted through comic strips, complete with dialogue—in the office: "That duplicating machine has broken down again! If we don't get a modern

---

1932: *Clarence Lillyblade takes over the Chicago office . . . Newly elected President Franklin D. Roosevelt's New Deal program stresses federal support of the economy . . . Dashiell Hammett publishes* The Thin Man *. . . RCA demonstrates electronic TV . . . Amelia Earhart is the first woman to fly alone across the Atlantic . . . Radio City Music Hall opens in New York City.*

machine we'll never get the work out" and in the home, "Oh Dear! It's out of order." For many industries there are specialized pictorial presentations, such as "The Invisible Market for Advertising Novelties," which depicts businessmen discovering a need for badges and souvenirs or neon signs. In addition, it provides a great deal of user survey information, said to be based on 100,000 calls in many different cities, organized to permit easy reference to a particular product or service.

In the accompanying guide, entitled "Selling the Eye as Well as the Ear," Lillyblade provides nine pages of detailed suggestions on how to use the material in "The Road to the Invisible Market." The purpose, he explains is to provide something for visual demonstration other than the directory itself. Pictures and statistics forcefully presented, he argues, can convey the facts about directory usage "better than the most 'silver tongued' salesman could ever do with words alone." Though he was himself a salesman-performer *par excellence,* Lillyblade was also an exponent of the idea that Donnelley's success required not a talented group of actors but a highly-trained professional sales force. [10]

A Loose-Knit Company

Donnelley's directory organization was divided into three distinct and distinctive regions in the 1930s, presided over by three strong, individualistic regional vice presidents—Clarence Lillyblade in Chicago, Raymond Gunnison in New York, and Arthur Bamforth in Philadelphia. As president of the corporation, George Overton allowed the regional heads to operate independently, and there was no overarching structure to impose centralization or even to facilitate interaction among the salesmen of the different regions. In 1936, Overton convened an unusual meeting

---

1933: The Donnelley Manual of Directory Salesmanship, *the first training guide, nears completion . . . Prohibition is repealed by the Twenty-first Amendment to the Constitution . . . Mae West utters her classic "Come up and see me some time" in the film "She Done Him Wrong" . . . President Franklin D. Roosevelt begins his radio broadcast "fireside chats" . . . Adolf Hitler is appointed Chancellor of Germany.*

1936: *Clarence Lillyblade's creativity produces the first fullfledged sales aids for the company . . . FDR and John Nance Garner are re-elected President and Vice President . . . Margaret Mitchell publishes* Gone With the Wind, *her only book . . . Henry Luce publishes* Life Magazine *. . . The Baseball Hall of Fame is established in Cooperstown, New York . . . King Edward VIII abdicates the throne when the British government opposes his marriage to the American Mrs. Wallis Warfield Simpson.*

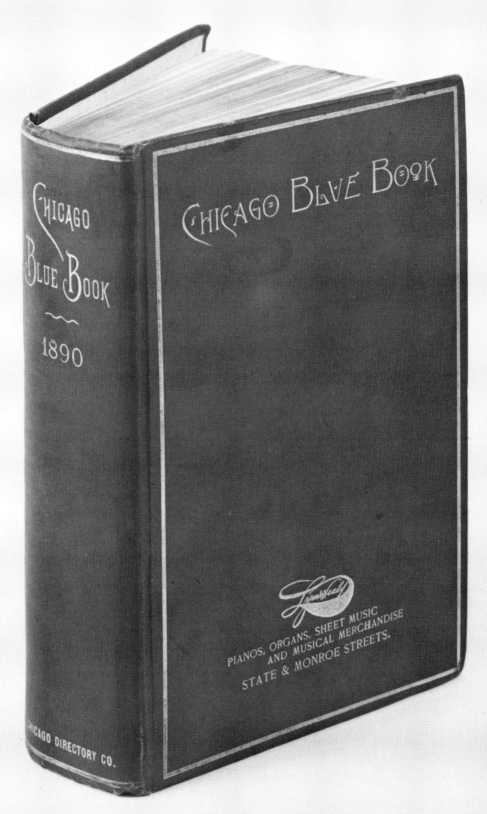

Chicago Blue Book, 1890
(Another early Donnelley publication)

Albert Von Hoffmann and Loren M. Berry
Two second generation pioneers in the
Directory Industry

in Rye, New York, of sales managers from every division and region of the company. Although the managers found a great deal of common ground and the meeting was widely judged a success, there was not to be another one until 1951.

Another short-lived project for coordinating directory activities in the regions was the creation of the position of Sales Observer, to be staffed by one man in Illinois, one in Pennsylvania, and two in New York. Their task was to observe and evaluate every salesman in the field, making daily reports and a final summary report for the region. It was intended that they would then switch regions and repeat the procedure, but the program was discontinued in 1937 when the initial survey was completed. The wealth of information it had generated was used independently in each region to develop training materials, and the regions continued to evolve separately.[11]

The operations of the three regions were shaped by many factors, the most important of which were the nature of their markets, their relationships to client telephone companies, and the personalities of the vice presidents who ran them.

Clarence O. Lillyblade: Chicago

The Chicago Office benefited, of course, from Clarence Lillyblade's directory salesmanship, but it also had the advantage of being associated with the family printing firm, R. R. Donnelley & Sons, one of the oldest and most prestigious companies in the city, bearing the name of one of the most respected Chicago families. In the mid-1930s the Reuben H. Donnelley Corporation was not as close as it had once been to R. R. Donnelley & Sons—the annual company picnics were no longer held jointly, and Reuben H. Donnelley now had its own publication, *The Donnelley Advertiser,* for the Illinois region. Yet T. E. Donnelley, President of R. R. Donnelley & Sons, was also Chairman of the Board of Reuben H. Donnelley, and, with few exceptions, the stockholders of both companies were Donnelley family members. In the public eye the two companies were always closely linked together.[12]

Donnelley's prominence in Chicago enabled it to compete strongly for talented people in the field of advertising, and, as Reuben Donnelley himself had perceived so clearly, the Chicago marketplace was fertile ground for salesmen to work in. By the 1930s, there were separate city and suburban directories in Chicago, as well as a number of "neighborhood" directories, and the telephone directory was firmly established as an advertising medium. Moreover, since Donnelley had been publishing telephone directories for so long, its relationship with Illinois Bell was equally well established. The possibility of losing a contract was always in the background, of course, but there was a strong tradition of cooperation in the spirit of a partnership of equals. This created a supportive environment for innovators such as Lillyblade and for all the Donnelley salesmen in this region. For all of these reasons, the experience gained in selling directory advertising in Chicago was unique within the Donnelley organization, and, for much of the company's history, the salesmen there enjoyed an advantage over their colleagues in other regions, thanks to that experience.

Raymond M. Gunnison: New York

In New York, the Reuben H. Donnelley Corporation was not a directory publisher but the sales agent for New York Telephone Company. The region encompassed the various upstate New York directories, the downstate *Manhattan Red Book,* and, after 1910, separate classified directories for the Bronx, Brooklyn, and Queens. The downstate section was expanded further in 1930 by contracts covering Long Island and Westchester County. This was also a rich marketplace, although it was more difficult to canvass. Each of the metropolitan boroughs had its own directory, so that selling to large-scale advertisers was very complex. And there were also logistical problems arising from differences between the boroughs and the difficulty of travel within the metropolis. Recruitment of salespeople was also more difficult in New York City because there were so many other strong advertising firms offering employment. It was difficult to manage the New York region as a whole because upstate and downstate were so different and so separate, in contrast to Illinois, where Chicago enjoyed an overwhelming predominance and a tradition of leadership and control.

For more than a decade, the Vice President in charge of the New York region was Raymond M. Gunnison, who later became President of the corporation. Gunnison came to Donnelley in 1929 after serving as owner-publisher of *The Brooklyn Eagle.* He was recruited by T. E. Donnelley, who, as Chairman of the Board after his brother's death, had taken it upon himself to see that the regional operations were under proven leadership. Gunnison made his mark upon the corporation almost immediately by negotiating the purchase of its first trade journal, *The National Cleaner and Dyer.* With this stroke he established, in 1931, the Trade Papers Division of Reuben H. Donnelley. Under his leadership this division was expanded with the acquisition of *The Starchroom Laundry Journal* in 1934, *The Ice Cream Trade Journal* and *The Spotting Manual of the Dry Cleaning Industry* in 1937, and, also for the dry cleaning industry, *The Fur Book,* in 1950. Thus, Gunnison reestablished publishing as a part of the Donnelley business, a part that would remain a vital, though minor division of the corporation for over four decades.

Gunnison was not, however, as dynamic a leader in the directory field. Responsibility for the sales operation in New York generally devolved upon lower levels of management, and the salesmen were left to develop their own, highly individualistic styles and methods. As Clarence Lillyblade demonstrated, a flamboyant style could be an asset in selling, and this was certainly true in the tough New York environment. In the 1930s, for example, Joe Silverberg made his reputation by wearing, without fail, a white carnation in his lapel. In the winter, he also wore white gloves and a white scarf, and he was long remembered in Manhattan as "the man from the yellow pages with the white flower." He was a good salesman and contributed much to the Donnelley organization. Yet even Lillyblade had some difficulty with telephone company officials who thought him ultra-modern, and the management of the New York Telephone Company tended to look askance at such individualism within the directory sales force. They took to sending observers to every Donnelley sales rally and sometimes out in the field. It was difficult to maintain a good working relationship and high performance under these conditions.[13]

Arthur H. Bamforth: Philadephia

In 1930, the Philadelphia office became the center of the third region of the Donnelley directory operation, taking on contracts with Bell of Pennsylvania, the Diamond State Telephone Company, also of Pennsylvania, and the Chesapeake and Potomac Telephone Company (C & P) of West Virginia. After that, it expanded rapidly. In 1931, contracts were negotiated with Bell for eastern Pennsylvania and Delaware—making this the "Penn/Delaware" Region—and also with an independent firm, the Lehigh Telephone Company. In 1933 it took over publication of the Philadelphia classified directory, in 1936 of the Bell directories for central Pennsylvania, and in 1947 of the Pittsburgh classified.

Despite the rapid growth in numer of directories, Penn/Delaware was the most deprived of the regions in terms of its advertising market, which, outside of Philadelphia and Pittsburgh, was sparsely populated and, largely undeveloped. In addition, it suffered similar problems to those in New York, resulting from the separateness of its subregions, one centered around Pittsburgh, the other around Philadelphia.

For the first 20 years, this region was under the leadership of Arthur H. Bamforth. Indeed, it was Bamforth who was responsible for its existence as a directory organization, for when he arrived in Philadelphia that office was handling little more than delivery, warehousing, and window display installations. On his own initiative, he made a case to the telephone companies in his region and, after winning contracts for a few directories, continued to court Bell of Pennsylvania, gradually expanding the region to take in most of the state. He also secured the contract from the C & P Telephone Company for its West Virginia region, and when the C & P Vice President for West Virginia became President, Bamforth convinced him to turn over to Donnelley the directories of the remaining three C & P divisions—Virginia, Maryland, and Washington, D. C. Thus, Bamforth was also largely responsible for the creation of Donnelley's fourth directory region.[14]

An experienced salesman and knowledgeable in the directory business, Bamforth was unusually formal in dealing with his staff. In New York, Gunnison was known generally as "Ray," in Chicago "Clarence was just Clarence," but in Philadelphia it was always "Mr. Bamforth," who insisted on addressing everyone else formally as well. All Donnelley salesmen were required to wear jackets, ties, and hats on customer calls at this time, but in Penn/Delaware the dress code prevailed in the office as well, and transgression could be a firing offense. This rigid formality was a negative influence in an organization depending so heavily for success on the sustained commitment and enthusiasm of its sales force. Moreover, the compensation scale in this region was lower than in others. These factors are reflected to some degree in the relatively erratic performance of the Penn/Delaware Region during much of the Bamforth era, as shown in Figure 1.

Despite these regional differences, all of Donnelley's directory operations expanded during the decade of the 1930s as the nation's economy gradually regained its health. By 1940, the company's revenues from directory sales had increased by 88 percent over the level of 1934, and its profit from

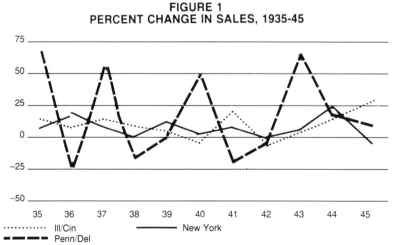

FIGURE 1
PERCENT CHANGE IN SALES, 1935-45

············ Ill/Cin   ——— New York
▬ ▬ ▬ Penn/Del

Source: Calculated from J.C. Walker, "Historical Financial Data," "Telephone Directory Division (Excluding National Yellow Pages, Compilation, and Street Address)."

these sales had increased by over 200 percent. In 1942, George Overton died, Raymond Gunnison succeeded him as President of Reuben H. Donnelley, to preside over an era of continuing growth in the business.[15]

The War Brings Changes

The war years brought a number of potentially serious problems. The draft posed severe difficulties in staffing, as none of Donnelley's activities was considered a vital industry. The year 1942 was a terrible one for the Direct Mail Division. Compilation of the automobile owners' list was discontinued and, early the following year, the board of directors tentatively decided to abandon the Nevada, Iowa, branch, which primarily handled mailings based on that list. The Directory Division did better, but was encountering rising costs due to inflation. In addition, unions had been formed in both Philadelphia and New York, and the company faced arbitration by the War Labor Board over contracts that demanded not only wage increases but also union control of hiring, firing, and work assignments.[16]

By the end of 1943, however, most of these problems had been resolved. In the Direct Mail office, special wartime contracts for packing toothbrushes, rolling bandages, making hairnets, and packaging sutures provided sustaining revenue, and a few new, major marketing contracts pushed profits in some offices to all-time highs. Not only was the Nevada plant kept open, but much of the business from the Chicago office was moved there, as Iowa was outside the declared critical labor area. The Distribution Division also began to grow rapidly, and directory delivery was separated from so-called commercial delivery, or merchandise distribution, which was developing into more of a marketing than a distribution service.[17]

Although the Philadelphia union was disbanded, the New York contract dispute remained very much alive before the War Labor Board. Gunnison reported to the directors early in 1944 that this was a critical juncture for Donnelley in the directory field. If the union won the right to control assignments, the company's position as manager of the sales force would be irreparably weakened and its relationship with the telephone company seriously jeopardized. Yet, Gunnison noted, "if we are successful in proving this is not a case for union organization we will probably have the problem behind us for all times."[18]

The outcome was much as Gunnison hoped, though not through the decision of the War Labor Board, whose ruling was that Donnelley had to accept the disputed contract. This decision was effectively overruled by President Roosevelt, who failed to sign it. In the absence of a signed directive, Donnelley management in New York continued to operate as before and was able to resolve the dispute internally.

By the end of the year, the sales force had voted the union out. It was a year filled with drama, during which T. E. Donnelley, nearly 80 years old, went to Washington during the hearings to emphasize the importance of the issue, and Donnelley's counsel, Curtiss E. Frank, filed with the White House a lengthy brief for the President's consideration, citing precedents for overturning the War Labor Board's ruling dating back to the Civil War. After this, the result was something of an anticlimax, but it was of great significance for the company. Two decades later, beginning in New York, Donnelley would undergo an intense, management-driven professionalization of its sales force that would bring it to a position of leadership in the industry. A critical precondition for this improvement would be the absence of a union.

Another important development during the war years was the creation of telephone sales departments. As a matter of necessity, many directory salesmen had come to rely on the telephone to make contact with less promising prospects, particularly after the wartime rationing of gasoline made car travel more difficult. Due to the extreme labor shortages caused by the draft, Donnelley, like most employers of the time, increasingly hired women, and area managers organized telephone sales units to which many of the women were assigned. Prior to the war, the sales effort had been focused exclusively on bringing in expensive ads. Telephone sales opened up a new source of revenue from small-value ads, such as doctors' listings of specialties or hours of business. Most of the so-called "premise sales" positions were taken back by men after the war, but the telephone sales groups remained, with women a permanent part of Donnelley's directory sales force.[19]

All of these wartime developments had a lasting impact on the company, but the most important change in the directory business to come out of the war years happened outside of Donnelley in the society at large. This change began with wartime shortages, which made necessary goods and services difficult to find. It was fostered by the dislocation of families during the war and by the great mobility of the generation that started

---

1940: *The Company's revenues from directory sales rise by more than 200% . . . President Roosevelt asks Congress for $1,800,000 for defense . . . Wendell L. Willkie is nominated for President by the Republican Party in June; in November, President Roosevelt is re-elected with 449 electoral votes to Willkie's 82 . . . F. Scott Fitzgerald dies of a heart attack at age 44, in Hollywood . . . Color television is demonstrated over the Columbia Broadcasting System's New York City station.*

families and careers at the war's end. It was supported by the spread of the telephone into 60 percent of all U. S. households by 1949, by the concurrent diffusion of the new dial telephone technology, and, not least, by the changeover to a rate system offering unlimited local calls to most users. Finally, it was powered by the postwar surge of productivity and prosperity that created a vast array of consumer goods and brought them within the reach of the great American middle class. What resulted in the end was the acceptance of the classified telephone directory as an integral part of the market system. In the public eye, it became an essential source of information for consumers and an indispensable form of advertising for most businesses.

Donnelley salesmen returning to their jobs after the war found their profession transformed. Whereas before they had had to use every conceivable argument to convince customers of the value of directory advertising, increasingly they found themselves preaching to the converted. They were also receiving more assistance than ever before from the telephone company. AT&T's National Trade Mark Service demonstrated to local business people that the medium was valued by national companies, and magazine advertising that included the slogan "Look for Your Local Dealer in the Classified Directory" suggested how businesses would benefit from directory advertising. In addition, AT&T expanded its program of user surveys and began to advertise its directory services more aggressively. The net result of these changes was an upward surge in directory advertising sales paralleling an increase in national annual retail sales of roughly 200 percent within a decade of the war's end.[20]

Postwar Problems

The future looked bright for the directory advertising industry in 1946, and Donnelley appeared to be in an excellent position to make the most of the opportunities that lay on the horizon. The company had been in the business for 60 years, longer than any other sales organization, and it had already taken significant steps toward professionalizing its operations. Yet, there were weaknesses in the Directory Division that prevented Donnelley from taking off as it might have done in the postwar years. The separation of the regions and the insularity that resulted from this had a stultifying effect and prevented the diffusion of many of Lillyblade's innovations—and those of others as well. With no corporate direction or support, area and district managers were unable to do much in the way of training. And without training, Lillyblade's sales aids were relatively useless.

Another impediment was the attitude of Donnelley's president, Raymond Gunnison, toward the directory business. His views are clearly expressed in the statement, made in February 1943, in which he explained to the board of directors why directory managers were the only ones in the corporation not to be compensated on the basis of their departments' earnings. This policy and the outlook behind it undoubtedly damaged the directory operation in the mid-1940s.

> The situation in regard to the telephone directory advertising is different from our other departments [e.g. Direct Mail, Trade Papers] because the business is built around contracts with the Telephone Company, and the Donnelley history—our reputation—is an important factor. Because of the similarity of our operations, men are readily transferred from one job to another, and, therefore, are not as vital as in other departments. For this reason it does not seem necessary to have the same standards of compensation.[21]

The situation took a turn for the worse when the Bell companies of New York and Pennsylvania began to examine their long-standing relationships with Donnelley. In Chicago and New York, Reuben Donnelley had negotiatied agreements whereby his company would receive as profit 5 percent of gross directory revenues. This amounted to a commission of about 25 percent. As revenues began to rise, however, New York Telephone began to fear that Donnelley's profits would be too great and requested a complete accounting of costs and profits in the New York Region. As a result of its study, the telephone company reduced Donnelley's commission to 23 percent in 1947. At the same time, competitors, particularly L. M. Berry, were offering services at commission rates as low as 21 percent. In 1948, Berry and Donnelley were going head-to-head for the business of the C & P Telephone Company. Donnelley was able to carry the day with C & P, but only at a 23 percent commission. "We were able to sell them on the idea that we were 2% better than Berry," Gunnison reported to the

---

1942: *Raymond Gunnison becomes President, on the death of George Overton . . . The draft makes staffing difficult; unions are formed in Philadelphia and New York . . . The French passenger liner* Normandie *burns in New York Harbor . . . General MacArthur is made Commander of Allied Forces in the Southwest Pacific . . . James Thurber's* My World and Welcome to It *includes the tale "The Secret Life of Walter Mitty."*

1944: *Labor difficulties end, and T.E. Donnelley, nearly 80 years old, goes to Washington . . . U.S. planes bomb Berlin for the first time . . . Tennessee Williams publishes* The Glass Menagerie, *his first successful work . . . Bing Crosby stars in the film* Going My Way. . . . *Theodore von Karman, "Father of the Supersonic Age," helps establish the Jet Propulsion Laboratory in California . . . Oswald Avery proves that DNA is the genetic material responsible for heredity.*

FIGURE 2
DONNELLEY DIRECTORY SALES, 1934-1954
(Millions)

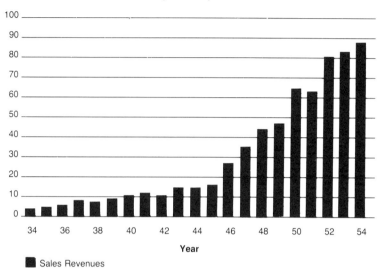

■ Sales Revenues

Source: J.C. Walker, "Historical Financial Data," "Telephone Directory Division (Excluding National Yellow Pages, Compilation, and Street Address)" for 1934-1945; and "Operating Division Sales and Operating Profit" for 1946-1954.

board, "but to claim an advantage of 4% would have been impossible." This experience led the company, in an effort to further improve relationships with its telephone company clients, to offer to reduce its commission in other regions as well. Illinois Bell and Cincinnati Bell chose to continue their existing agreements, but Bell of Pennsylvania accepted Donnelley's offer.[22]

These concessions marked the beginning of the worst years in the history of Donnelley's directory operation. In both New York and Penn/Delaware, most of the advances that had been made in the previous decade were rolled back as costs were cut to maintain profits of 5 percent at the lower rate of commission. Expenditures for training and sales support were severely reduced or eliminated, and the quality of office accommodations and general working conditions rapidly deteriorated as rental and maintenance costs were cut back. Moreover, reductions in compensation led to an extremely high turnover of the sales force and, in general, to a lowering of the quality of personnel in this all-important area. These policies severely injured the company's overall performance. Despite the strong upward trend of directory revenues in the postwar period, Donnelley's gains from year to year were erratic, at best, as Figure 2 shows. In Penn/Delaware the situation was made worse after 1949 by the fact that the operations in the new C & P region diverted Bamforth's attention and were a severe drain on sales and management talent. This region would remain a troubled one for almost 20 years.[23]

The C & P Region

In contrast, the C & P region, after a few very difficult and profitless canvasses, was the company's star for many years. In large part this was due to the camaraderie that developed within the group of selected Donnelley salesmen and managers assembled in 1949. Throughout most of the first months, the district managers almost never had dinner at home, but sold advertising all day and returned to the office at night to process their orders. Around midnight, most nights the general manager came around with coffee and sandwiches.[24]

Even after the pressure diminished, the managers of C & P remained close and were able to maintain friendly relationships with directory employees at all levels, partly because the regional operation was much smaller than the other three. The four regional groups of the C & P Telephone Company—Virginia, West Virginia, Maryland, and Washington, D.C.—functioned almost as separate companies, and customer relationships had to be carefully nurtured with each of them. But, with the exception of West Virginia, the C & P market was a good one, with many developing suburban areas. The *esprit de corps* that existed among the managers fostered a healthy competitiveness with the more established Donnelley regions, and many new ideas were tried out in C & P that later were adopted as major innovations, companywide.

V

The Harrington Era
(1951–1961)

David L. Harrington became President of the Reuben H. Donnelley Corporation when Raymond Gunnison was elected Chairman of the Board. Harrington had been a Vice President since 1943, and, by 1951, he had already set into motion some of the changes that were to be the hallmark of the decade of his presidency. His predecessor, a deeply rooted New Yorker, had refused to move to Chicago, so that Harrington, as Vice President, had been managing the head office for some time. As Chairman of the executive committee of the board of directors, he initiated a program to standardize accounting procedures throughout the corporation—a necessary first step toward any degree of centralization. He also started a program at the corporate level to develop sales promotion ideas that could be used in various offices, and he called a National Trade Mark conference to begin standardizing procedures in this area of directory sales. In addition, he convened a so-called "accuracy meeting" so that the regions could share their ideas on this critical issue, and a meeting of regional personnel managers to consider standard practices for hiring and training. Out of the latter meeting came a job evaluation program, encompassing all employees, and a "Standard Personnel Practices Manual" for use in hiring.[1]

On assuming the title of President, Harrington continued his drive to unify what had become four very separate and independent regional operations. Over the years, they all had developed their own procedures and standards, and the results that they produced were very uneven. In order to begin to establish a single high standard of performance, it was necessary to break down the intense regionalism that had developed unchecked for two decades.

The Beginning of Unification

A three-day conference in 1951 brought together all the regional directory general sales managers to meet each other and to share their expertise, and this became an annual affair. Another measure aimed at unification was the creation of a new internal publication, "The Sales Round-Up." Each region produced its own monthly magazine under this title, all carrying an insert, "Head Office Briefs," which covered corporate news and features designed to familiarize the different divisions and regions with each other.[2]

In September 1951, Harrington revived the service organization, defunct since Reuben Donnelley's death, for employees who had been with the company 25 years or more, and he renamed it the Quarter Century Club. Some 70 individuals with service ranging from 25 to 53 years were honored at luncheons at which they were presented with gold emblems and certificates. Their names were inscribed on wooden plaques that were mounted in the entrance halls of each of the regional headquarters. The following year, the Donnelley Service Club was created to recognize employees with five or more years of service. "In my opinion," Harrington told the board of directors, "these different plans for improving the morale of our people are among our most outstanding achievements."[3]

By 1953, these two service organizations encompassed about 1,000 employees, and luncheons were held for them in New York, Pittsburgh, Philadelphia, Chicago, Los Angeles, Cincinnati, Nevada, Iowa, and Terre Haute, Indiana—which had only been in the company for five years. One of the most significant aspects of the luncheons was that David Harrington attended almost every one of them and continued to do so annually as long as he was at the head of Donnelley. Indeed, his determination to go everywhere and to meet everyone in the company was probably the most striking aspect of his personal managerial style, and it soon became a managerial style of Reuben H. Donnelley and an important part of the process of unification.

The drive to centralize continued with the appointment of a corporate controller, who was charged with completing the standardization of accounting procedures, and of a staff methods and systems manager, who was to help with all systems problems from job evaluation to directory publication. Equally important, however, was the effort to improve management within the Directory Division itself and to identify and promote capable leaders within the corporation. Harrington lamented the "altogether" too many instances where men have been put into management positions because of a fine sales record, only to find that they are definitely not qualified for management positions."[4]

One of his first steps as President was to bring into the firm an outsider, Edward A. O'Rorke, a business-school graduate with a well-established career in corporate management. After briefly "learning the ropes" in directory sales, O'Rorke moved quickly into key management positions, and, early in 1953, he was appointed General Manager of the New York

Directory Publications Division. On a broader scale, Harrington addressed the problem of management by having every prospective management appointee tested by an outside consultant, and soon there was a management development program under which potential leaders were recruited from the outside and trained in directory sales, while the most promising current managers in each region were sent to management school.[5]

In February 1954, Harrington brought Schuyler Hoslett into the company from the Columbia School of Management, and Hoslett started right to work developing a training program for district managers and planning an organization development program structured around seminars and the case-study method of analyzing management problems. Throughout the early 1950s, there was a continual movement of upper-level managers in the Directory Division. In February of 1956, Harrington reported with relief on the progress of his management programs: "Today, for the first time in five years, we can look forward to a year in our Directory Publications Division in which we will not be faced with some serious management crisis."[6]

Resolving Regional Problems

In fact, for the first five years of David Harrington's presidency, Donnelley's Directory Division had been in an almost constant state of crisis. The new C & P region continued to grow and prosper, and Illinois-Cincinnati seemed to sail along with relative ease—in 1951 the Chicago *Red Book* was the first classified directory in the nation to surpass $10 million in annual revenue. But problems in Penn/Delaware and metropolitan New York cast these achievements into shadow. The ill effects of several years of neglect were clearly reflected in the poor sales results of these two regions.

In downstate New York, the crisis had several facets. Beginning in 1947, Donnelley and several Bell companies had been embroiled in a $48 million lawsuit brought by the Oleck Directory Company, which had attempted to establish competing "green books" in the New York directory

1951: *David L. Harrington, Vice President since 1943, becomes President of the Reuben H. Donnelley Corporation as Raymond Gunnison is elected Chairman of the Board . . . The Quarter Century Club is revived . . . The Chicago Red Book is the first classified directory to surpass $10 million in annual revenue . . . James Jones publishes* From Here to Eternity *. . . The first transcontinental television broadcast is President Truman's address at the Japanese Peace Conference in San Francisco . . . Employment of women reaches a new high, greater even than during World War II.*

market. The lawyer handling this case, for Donnelley was Curtiss E. Frank, who had presented the company's case before the War Labor Board several years before. Frank was a partner in the law firm of Charles Evans Hughes and had been an assistant U. S. attorney in the southern district of New York and the mayor of Yonkers. In addition, he was an acquaintance of Raymond Gunnison, who recruited him into the company as Vice President and General Counsel in September 1949. Within a few months, Frank found himself General Manager of the New York Directory Division, because the previous incumbent had suffered a debilitating stroke. In his predecessor's desk he found a consultant's report on the condition of the downstate operation that was truly devastating, and this was his rather harsh introduction into the directory business. [7]

Clarence Lillyblade was immediately dispatched from Chicago to give Curtiss Frank a crash course in classified sales and management. Yet it was Frank himself who determined how to deal with a very dissatisfied New York Telephone Company and with an equally dissatisfied and unproductive sales force. His approach, not unlike Harrington's, was to get out and meet people. In addition to cultivating friendly relationships with phone company executives, he personally visited the homes of his salesmen to talk to them and to their wives about the importance of improving their performance. Frank's experience and skill in politics served him well in this circumstance, and through mediation, encouragement, and selective firing and hiring, he succeeded in producing, by 1951, a 12 percent gain in the Manhattan classified directory and an 18 percent gain in Brooklyn. [8]

Perhaps even more important, Frank, with Harrington's backing, succeeded in winning the cooperation of New York Telephone in addressing the terrible problem of records management for the downstate directories. In 1950, the New York office was virtually buried beneath unprocessed orders, sales reports, and salesmen's account records, and an accountant hired to standardize procedures throughout Donnelley had to spend most of his time helping out with this morass in New York. The following year the company asked a consulting firm, Booz, Allen & Hamilton, to design a mechanized system to manage the New York directory records, and New York Telephone agreed to spend dollar for dollar with Donnelley in this project.

Just before Christmas, 1952, as the process of conversion was under way, the consulting project manager collapsed. There were 18,000 orders for the Brooklyn classified directory still to be processed, and the book was due to go to press on January 2. In this crisis, T. E. Donnelley's sons, Gaylord, who had just suceeded Gunnison as Chairman of the Reuben H. Donnelley board, and Elliott, lent the support of the family printing firm, R. R. Donnelley & Sons, sending one of their best young engineers to New York to assist in managing the project. David Harrington quickly assembled a force of 40 women from every region of the company—the best compilation department that Donnelley could provide—and Curtiss Frank arranged for this crew to be housed in the Gramercy Park Hotel. They put the Brooklyn book to bed and stayed on into the spring to help with the Manhattan *Red Book* as well. "I . . . want to mention the splendid co-operation given to New York by all of our Directory Divisions," Harrington told his board of directors that February. "This spirit of team work and co-operation is something that did not exist in this Corporation only a short time ago, and I am very proud of this new spirit that is so evident today."[9]

After this crisis, Harrington made clear to the board that he intended to reverse the policy on directory profits that had been in effect since the reduction in commissions. He was willing to invest profits in the short-run to improve the performance of directory operations, as this had fallen well below the standard prevailing in the Bell System. This new policy paid immediate dividends in good will from New York Telephone, and Curtiss Frank was able to negotiate a one-year extension on Donnelley's contract, due to expire on April 1, 1953. At the same time, the telephone company agreed to support an "all-out make-up campaign for 1953" by granting rate increases, by stepping up its public campaign promoting directory usage, and by providing significant funding for a special program that was to include added training and supervision of salesmen, incentive contests and prizes, better coverage of the so-called "fringe market," and increased production of speculative copy and other promotional materials that could be given to prospective advertisers. These measures succeeded in producing in the New York metropolitan area as a whole an account gain of 13 percent and a revenue gain of 24.4 percent. As an added bonus, Frank settled the Oleck suit, ending the challenge to Donnelley's primacy in the New York directory market.[10]

At the victory dinner, held to celebrate the closing of the 1953 directories, the president of New York Telephone announced his company's willingness to enter a new 10-year contract with Reuben H. Donnelley at a more favorable rate of commission. There was still a long way to go to make up the ground lost between 1947 and 1950. But the all-important first step had been taken with the commitment to a program of significant investment in directory operations.

A similar commitment had to be made in the Penn/Delaware region, where the maintenance of profits despite a cut in commission rate had had much the same effect as in New York. In 1953, the Chicago office had to assist the Philadelphia canvass by sending down a dozen of its top salesmen, and even New York contributed some of its personnel to this effort. Directory officials at Bell of Pennsylvania were extremely unhappy with revenues, which, they pointed out, were some $2 million below what they would have been if growth had kept pace with the system average since 1948. "The amazing thing is," Harrington remarked, "that in spite of this record they express complete confidence in our ability to do a job for them." By that time, However, Donnelley had already begun to make signficant new investments in the regional operation and had proclaimed 1955 a "do-it-or-else" situation in Pennsylvania-Delaware:

> We are throwing into the operation all the top quality, experienced management people we can find—are going all-out in a training program—adding 25 or 30 people to the sales staff—and taking other steps that are expensive but which we believe will produce the results we know must be secured regardless of cost.[11]

With this big push the Penn/Delaware directories went from last place in sales gain among the Donnelley regions to first place.

Relations with AT&T

By the late 1950s, Donnelley's relationships with its telephone company clients were once again secure. This did not mean, however, that they were easy relationships. Within the directory industry as a whole, revenues were soaring—Bell System sales rose from less than $100 million in 1947 to over $300 million in 1957—and because of this, AT&T and all of its operating subsidiaries were beginning to scrutinize their directory operations more intensely. Frequent publication of comparative statistics on revenue per telephone in each directory facilitated comparisons, and Donnelley was criticized when any of its four regions failed to equal the system average. Donnelley executives could point to the fact that most of its major directories were in older, more stable market areas. But it was not really in their best interest to make excuses, since there were always those within AT&T who argued that the telephone companies could profitably take over Donnelley's business themselves. Thus, while within its regions the Directory Division had no competitors in the usual sense, there was always *implied* competition with the Bell System itself. "It would be misleading for me to leave the impression that everything is sunshine and light in our Directory operations," David Harrington told the board late in 1955. "The fact is that far too many Telephone Companies are doing a

---

1953: *The President of New York Telephone announces the Company's willingness to enter a new 10-year contract . . . Malenkov succeeds Stalin as Soviet Premier . . . Arthur Miller publishes* The Crucible, *about the Salem witch trials . . . Major Charles E. Yeager reaches an air speed record of more than 1600 mph.*

*The Donnelley Manual of Directory Salesmanship,
1950 and 1934 Editions*

A Variety of early Donnelley Directories

better job than we are in getting sales gains, and we are constantly being needled by AT&T and our own Telephone Company customers to do a better job."[12]

Around this time, AT&T began to take on more seriously the task of standardizing directories and promoting usage through public advertising. The cartoon character Wolley Segap (Yellow Pages spelled backward) made his debut in 1954, and in 1955 AT&T began using a single symbol to foster widespread familiarity with the directory medium—an open book with a telephone and the slogan, "Find It Fast in the Yellow Pages." As part of the effort to impose industry standards and to increase recognition of the product, AT&T required that all classified directories be printed on yellow paper. This was an unwelcome directive for those who worked on the Chicago *Red Book,* which had been printed on white paper with a red cover since 1915. But Donnelley salesmen went out in the field promoting "The Red Book with Yellow Pages." In 1958, AT&T designated the month of May as "Yellow Pages Booster Month," and all Donnelley employees wore lapel pins to tout the directory. After this promotional effort, there was an annual publicity drive, usually with some sort of sales gimmick, such as paper dresses or party materials, distributed to customers free of charge. All of these devices, in combination with a general rise in consumer activity, made the Yellow Pages one of the most frequently consulted reference books in the country, and classified advertising in it, one of the best values.[13]

Perhaps in recognition of this success, the Bell System companies began to allow rate increases in most of their directories in the late 1950s. Between increased usage, which made it easier to sell advertising, and increased rates, which made each sale more profitable, it became almost impossible not to post significant revenue gains. Yet the pressure to perform remained intense, as competition within the system challenged Donnelley to produce sales gains to match those created by higher rates.

In February 1956, David Harrington became Chairman of the Board and Chief Executive Officer of Reuben H. Donnelley, and Curtiss Frank became President, moving to Chicago to assume that responsibility. Together Harrington and Frank continued to work at building an organization capable of meeting the competition. Their success in the effort was uneven. Illinois/Cincinnati, C & P, and upstate and suburban New York did well, while metropolitan New York and Penn/Delaware remained troubled regions with erratic results, as they struggled to make headway in difficult market areas and continued to suffer the ill effects of long years of underdevelopment. In 1960, there was an all-out "bootstrap canvass" in Brooklyn, and the same in Manhattan and the Bronx in 1961.[14]

Organizational Changes

From beginning to end, the "Harrington Era" was both a period of tremendous growth and a time of continual struggle for the Directory Division. But many good things came out of that struggle. For example, there was a major push to develop training programs at all levels. In 1953 the position of national sales coordinator and training manager was created. Soon after, each region established its own training department staffed with specialized training managers who took over from the district sales managers much of the responsibility for training that had previously been theirs. At the same time, there was a move to establish a system of field observation so that performance could be continually evaluated after the initial training period was over. Better management of directory records made it possible to provide better prospect information, and there was continual improvement in the quality of sales support material available. By 1957, Donnelley was providing its sales representatives with a newly developed "Sales Kit System" that included such aids as testimonial letters, usage study results, and sample advertising copy. Training and field observation then focused on the problem of getting people to use this wealth of material. [15]

The continuing thrust to improve management produced other important developments in this decade. Training programs were initiated and expanded at every level, from first-line district sales managers to regional vice presidents. Similarly, recruitment was intense at every level. In addition, as Harrington and Frank struggled to solve the problems in the Directory Division, they initiated a policy of creating positions at the corporate level in which individuals who had proven themselves in one region could bring their expertise to bear on the problems of all regions. This policy effected a diffusion of talent and ideas previously unknown in the organization, and it also served to open up opportunities to aspiring managers that had not existed before. Formerly they could never have expected to move beyond the boundaries of their own regional hierarchies. [16]

As President, Curtiss Frank persuaded the stockholders, primarily the members of the Donnelley family, to reorganize the company to make

---

1954: *Wolley Segap makes his debut . . . The U.S. Senate censures Senator Joseph McCarthy . . . The* Nautilus, *the world's first nuclear powered submarine, is launched . . . Ernest Hemingway receives the Nobel Prize in Literature . . . The United States authorizes the construction of the St. Lawrence Seaway in cooperation with Canada . . . Hurricane Carol causes $500 million in losses on Long Island and in New England.*

possible the sale of stock to key Donnelley managers. "It is of the utmost importance to the long time welfare of the Corporation" he argued, "that those on whom we are to rely for future corporate success be given an opportunity to have a proprietary interest in the Corporation." This statement, as well as the policy itself, clearly shows the central importance of management development in the corporate policy of this era.[17]

The appointment in 1957 of Donald R. Arnold to Operating Vice President of Directory Publication is an outstanding example of the creation of a new, superregional position in this period. Arnold had joined the company as a sales trainee in 1927 and had risen through the ranks to become Vice President of the Illinois/Cincinnati region. In his new position, he moved to New York, in order to be closer to the more troubled areas of the operation, and brought with him his assistant general manager in Illinois/Cincinnati, William W. Geary, as National General Sales Manager. In addition, he brought in from the outside a market research analyst as a member of his staff. With these appointments, he sought to upgrade management at the highest level, and, at the same time, he worked on improving morale throughout the organization by making physical improvements in sales offices and increasing the compensation of sales and sales management personnel.

In 1960, Arnold introduced a "comprehensive marketing concept," including innovations, such as new directory formats, the introduction of newly scoped directories, and new sales aids and training materials. Rather quickly these proposals became known to directory officials in the Bell System, and they were "enthusiastically received." Then Donnelley was invited to contribute two people to an AT&T task force to develop the details of the proposed National Yellow Pages Service (NYPS)—the kind of positive recognition the board was extremely pleased to see. Now they were able to contemplate the possibility that the corporation, already the largest independent directory organization, might begin to assume a more active leadership role in the industry. This was a welcome prospect, not just for its own sake but also because it would further cement Donnelley's position in the Bell System.[18]

Other Donnelley Businesses

The star performer of Donnelley in these years was Direct Mail, which had grown from a list department of two, in the Chicago Directory Company in 1914, to a division with 3,000 employees in 1955. The basic business of this division was to handle large-scale publicity mailings for national advertisers. Donnelley provided not only the labor and facilities for these undertakings but also the list of potential consumers to whom the mailings would be sent. The standard data base had long been the

National Car and Truck Owners' List. This had been compiled by the R. L. Polk Company, since before World War II under agreement with Reuben H. Donnelley, whereby Donnelley served as sales agent for the list.

Although the direct mail industry died out almost completely during the war, there were clear signs that it would resume afterwards at an even greater volume. Donnelley therefore developed a new list on a broader data base, the so-called Donnelley Occupant List, which made it possible to mail advertising material to every household without knowing who lived there. Once this list had been developed, Donnelley began to use other sources of information, primarily the U.S. Census, to establish the socioeconomic characteristics of different regions, districts, and even neighborhoods, so that mailing campaigns could be targeted in a more sohpisticated way. Direct mail was a potentially volatile business that could suffer severe setbacks from increases in postal rates or an economic downturn affecting prospective advertisers. However, in many years this division, though it produced only about 20 percent of Donnelley's revenues, brought in as much as 40 percent or 50 percent of total corporate profits.[19]

One explanation for this success was the high level of management that Direct Mail enjoyed, beginning in 1922, when David Harrington and "Andy" Anderson began to rise within the division. Anderson was largely responsible for the establishment of the Direct Mail Creative Department in 1930. It was this department that spearheaded the transformation of Direct Mail from a simple mailing service and supplier of lists to a bona fide marketing division. Once that transformation had been made, Direct Mail offered significant opportunites for men with entrepreneurial and managerial skills. As the Vice President at the head of Direct Mail for eight years, Harrington showed the same intense drive to develop and promote capable managers that he later brought to the corporation as a whole.

Among the many strong men who came up through Direct Mail under Harrington's supervision were two who would succeed him as presidents of Donnelley—Hamilton B. Mitchell and Harrington E. Drake, Jr. Mitchell joined the corporation in 1939, worked for some time in both production and sales, and, by 1952, was manager of the New York Direct Mail office. Drake came to Donnelley in 1947 as a directory sales representative, but within a few years he moved over to sales in Direct Mail. He left the firm for four years to work in rural New Hampshire, but returned to Direct Mail in 1958, when he was sent to head up the office in Los Angeles. This was then a difficult area in which to work, because there were relatively few large, national packaged goods corporations in the western states. Yet, in 1959, the Los Angeles operation showed a profit for the first time in three years. In that year, Mitchell succeeded Andy Anderson as Executive Vice President for Direct Mail. [20]

For the most part, Donnelley's other divisions were also expanding and profitable in this period. The Street Address Directory business, first undertaken in Buffalo in 1929, added new contracts in upstate New York in the 1940s. In the 1950s, it had begun to publish directories in major metropolitan areas—New York in 1951, Philadelphia in 1952, and Chicago in 1953. The Distribution Division had been split in 1943, separating the delivery of directories from distribution of product samples and advertising flyers. The latter function had been given a new title, "Merchandising," with the intention that it would begin to develop more along marketing lines. The following year both Merchandising and Directory Delivery had come under the control of David Harrington. Although Gunnison noted pessimistically to the board that Donnelley had reached "the saturation point" in directory delivery, this had proved not to be the case. In the 1950s, this division was able to win a number of significant new contracts, particularly in the South, from telephone companies that had become dissatisfied with their previous suppliers.

The only exception to this general pattern of success was the City Guides Division, which was established in 1953 to promote a so-phisticated map-and-directory unit designed for public buildings as a kind of traveller's aid. Initially promising, this venture faltered, largely on the inability of the manufacturer to meet production demands, and the business was liquidated in 1956. [21]

Pressure to Diversify

Among the board and the stockholders of the corporation at this time was a growing concern over their reliance on a business that was itself dependent on the good will of contractual partners. In the late 1950s, the Directory Division's contribution to total revenues ranged from 55 percent to 68 percent, as Figure 3 shows. Moreover, some 30 percent of directory revenues came from the Chicago, Manhattan, and Philadelphia books, two of which were, or had been, focal points of dissatisfaction within AT&T. [22]

Although the reforms that David Harrington had effected in Directory Division management offered the hope of securing and expanding business in this area, the success of Direct Mail and the richness of its management talent increased the desire of the stockholders to see Donnelley expand and diversify. On the board at this time was Charles C. Haffner, Jr., a son-in-law of T. E. Donnelley and Chairman of the Board of R. R. Donnelley & Sons. Haffner had been a general during the war who had played a leading role in the Battle of the Bulge, and he was widely known as "General Haffner." It was the General who spoke most forcefully in favor

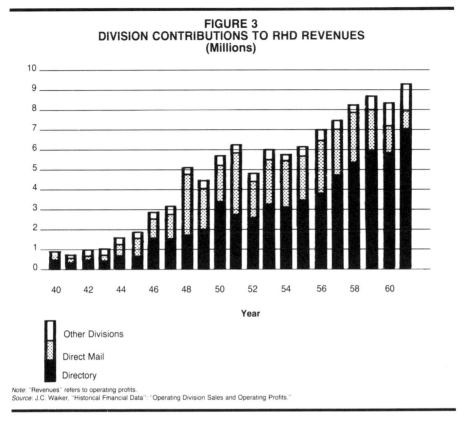

FIGURE 3
DIVISION CONTRIBUTIONS TO RHD REVENUES
(Millions)

Year

Other Divisions

Direct Mail

Directory

Note: "Revenues" refers to operating profits.
Source: J.C. Walker, "Historical Financial Data"; "Operating Division Sales and Operating Profits."

of diversification in the late 1950s. "Our organization is well staffed with many able young executives," he told David Harrington:

> It seems to me this base gives much promise of improving our services to our customers and to expand our business from them. But what seems of even greater importance now is that it gives us the possibility of aggressively expanding our business knowledge to other new but related fields.[23]

The Trade Papers Division had been expanding throughout the decade, purchasing *National Rug Cleaner* and *Oriental Rug Magazine* in 1952 and *Sports Age* in 1954. In 1955, it added four new publications through purchase of the Case-Sheppard-Mann Publishing Corporation, and, in 1959, it acquired the six medical and pharmaceutical journals of the Yorke Publishing Group. There had also been the abortive venture into city guides. In 1958, Donnelley had established a position that included responsibility for finding new business opportunities. Now, General Haffner was calling for expansion sufficient to reduce Donnelley's dependence on directory revenues down to 50 percent, and lower if possible, and he suggested that both Harrington and Frank devote significant portions of their time not just to expand existing nondirectory businesses, but "to comb out every available possible field on some organized systematic basis."[24] This directive was to drive Donnelley corporate policy for over a decade, but, in the short run, it was quickly overshadowed by the move to merge Reuben H. Donnelley with Dun & Bradstreet, Inc.

The Dun & Bradstreet Merger

The major stockholder in the corporation in 1960 was Reuben Donnelley's son, Thorne. A Navy test pilot with a distinguished record in World War I, Thorne had served as a Vice President of Reuben H. Donnelley from 1929 to 1947 and, since then, as a member of the board. He returned to the Navy during World War II, operating photographic laboratories, and, after the war, he purchased a Chicago radio station and was active in the communications field. Sixty-five years old in 1960, Thorne Donnelley was in failing health. Since Donnelley was not a public corporation, its stock was nonnegotiable. The directors recognized that this meant it would be extremely difficult to liquidate Thorne Donnelley's estate, as it had been to liquidate the estate of his father. Both the Donnelley heirs and the company would suffer in such a circumstance. It was not desirable, however, simply to go public, because this would require making public all the contracts on which the various sales divisions operated. Under these conditions, it was decided that the best course was to merge with a public corporation by means of an exchange of stock.[25]

Dun & Bradstreet, Inc. (D&B) emerged early on as the leading prospect. Created in 1933 by the merger of the R. G. Dun Corporation and The Bradstreet Company of Maine, D&B could trace its origins as a credit reporting business as far back as 1841. Since 1865, the centerpiece of that business had been a semiannual *Reference Book,* a directory of businesses providing statistics on their capital worth and general credit ratings. By 1960 D&B was publishing a variety of directories, including *The Million Dollar Directory, The Metalworking Directory,* and *The Boating Directory;* four "International Market Guides" covering countries in Europe and Latin America; and three magazines—*Dun's Review and Modern Industry, International Trade Review,* and *Service.*[26]

1956: *David Harrington becomes Chairman of the Board and Chief Executive Officer of the Reuben H. Donnelley Corporation . . . Senator Estes Kefauver defeats Senator John F. Kennedy for the Democratic vice-presidential nomination . . . Elvis Presley achieves national fame with the song "Heartbreak Hotel" . . . Michael DeBakey, a heart surgeon, introduces plastic tubing as replacements for diseased blood vessels . . . The first transatlantic telephone cable begins operation.*

In 1957, Donnelley had approached D&B to investigate the possibility of publishing an industrial directory together, and D&B came back with a proposal to pool the two companies' business paper interests. While neither of these schemes had worked out, it is clear that Donnelley and D&B had recognized each other as compatible partners. Moreover, as negotiations proceeded toward the merger, it became clear that the differences between the two corporations, as well as their similarities, made for a good fit. The credit-rating business was not dependent on contracts and was, therefore, more stable and solid than either directory or direct mail, but Donnelley could contribute an entrepreneurism that D&B lacked.[27]

In January 1961, Curtiss Frank became Chairman and Chief Executive Officer of Donnelley, and "Ham" Mitchell succeeded him as President and Chief Operating Officer. David Harrington became Chairman of Donnelley's Executive Committee, but, during the course of the search for Donnelley's corporate "marriage" partner Harrington fell ill, so that most of the responsibility for the negotiations fell upon Frank's shoulders. However, Kingman Douglass, a descendent of the Dun founders and a member of the D&B Board, was a long-time friend and associate of General Haffner. In their positions as directors of their respective companies, these two men made significant contributions to the successful conclusion of the merger.[28]

An exchange of Donnelley stock for the stock of Dun & Bradstreet was made on August 31, 1961, and on September 1 the Reuben H. Donnelley Corporation began to operate as a wholly-owned subsidiary of D&B. General Haffner, Gaylord Donnelley, Curtiss Frank, and Hamilton Mitchell joined the D&B Board of Directors, and Frank became Chairman of the D&B Executive Committee. In November the new Board made the symbolic gesture of holding its first meeting in Chicago, where Donnelley still maintained its head office. "I can't think of a more fitting way to launch our new merger," declared D&B Chairman, Wilson J. Newman, "than in Chicago, where both of these companies have operated so long and so successfully. After all, Chicago is the very heart of this country."[29]

David Harrington died on June 2, 1961, just weeks before the final agreement was made to merge the two companies. To a great extent it was his contributions to Donnelley that had made the merger possible. One of the important gains D&B expected to make from it, remarked Wilson Newman, was all the exciting, innovative Donnelley people. In addition, the changes that Harrington made had laid the foundation for even greater change *within* Donnelley in the years to come.[30]

VI
Building the Professional Sales Organization
(1962–1977)

As Chairman of Reuben H. Donnelley, Curtiss Frank continued to follow the program of "expansion and diversification" that had been the principal element of Donnelley's long-term strategy since the late 1950s, adding, among other things, the Life Extension Institute in 1969. On January 1, 1962, the Magazine Publishing Division purchased *The Constructor,* "the management magazine of the construction industry," and on April 1 it added *The Official Airline Guide.* This division expanded further in 1964 with the purchase of two international construction journals and the establishment of an International Publications Group. Diversification continued under Frank's successors with the acquisition of Telaflora Delivery Service in 1972 and Meisel Photochrome Corporation in 1974.[1]

Moreover, Frank and Mitchell, as President, continued to lead the company in the style established in the Harrington years, attending as many service club meetings, sales kick-off rallies, and victory dinners as it was possible to do. At the same time, however, many changes occurred within Donnelley that proved to be of great significance.

The Marketing Division

In the years immediately following the merger, the most dynamic division of the company continued to be Direct Mail. Following on the heels of a very bad year in 1961, there was a move to change the character of this division so that it would no longer be dependent entirely on direct mail but would provide "total marketing" services. To this end, in January 1962, Direct Mail and Merchandising were combined into a single unit— Donnelley Marketing. Subsequently this division pursued its own program of expansion through acquisition, adding in the early 1960s the Direct Mail Service of Omaha, Blum's Direct Advertising Agency of San Francisco, and *Motor Registration News.* In 1963, Donnelley entered into the direct mail industry in Europe, joining with new partners in the Netherlands and Great Britain. In the same year, the Marketing Division played the leading role in acquiring a 9.3 percent interest in the California firm, Subscription Television, an early venture into cable T.V. that was blocked at the start by the negative outcome of a California state referendum to allow subscription television.[2]

Not all of the growth in marketing came from the addition of new companies, however. One new project of this period was the Sel-A-Rama Service—a program of advertising films to be played in heavy-traffic commercial areas, such as banks. Another was the World of Beauty Club, begun in 1966, that sold cosmetics much as the Book of the Month Club sold books. Undoubtedly the most important new "product" of this period, however, was the Donnelley Quality Index. Since the 1930s, the Direct Mail Division had been using published statistics to define consumer markets. As the statistics produced by the U.S. Census Bureau and others became more refined, and as computers facilitated increasingly sophisticated analysis of these statistics, Donnelley was able to provide marketing advice on a totally different level from what it had previously offered.

All of these ventures and the revenues that they produced made the Marketing Division the "star" of the corporation, despite the fact that the Directory Division still earned close to 75 percent of total revenues. "Just as the Directory Division serves as the corporate breadbasket," Ham Mitchell told the Board in January 1964, "marketing must be called upon to wear the entrepreneurial hat and deliver the big gains . . . so that the Corporation as a whole can continue to show a respectable progress."[3]

The New York Telephone Company Contract

For the entrepreneurs in Donnelley, the Directory Division was not where the action was in the early 1960s. Nevertheless, changes were beginning then that would ultimately transform it into a very dynamic division. The company was still struggling with directories in its "core" cities, whose revenues were declining slightly while those in other areas rose. Don Arnold developed some new marketing strategies focused on making directories more useful to consumers as a means of boosting advertising sales. But Donnelley remained unable to make much headway against this problem and began to push on other fronts to maintain its standing in the Bell System.

After 1960, the company threw itself wholeheartedly into AT&T's new National Yellow Pages Service (NYPS), even though it was believed that this effort was hurting advertising sales in the big city directories. In addition, having made large expenditures to expand and improve its telephone sales units, Donnelley shared its new training program, "Dial To Dollars," with telephone company clients. Finally, in a move more symbolic than substantive, the company elevated its directory operation above divisional status, creating a new entity, the Reuben H. Donnelley Telephone Directory Company, and making Don Arnold its President. The headquarters of this new company was located in Chicago, thus softening the blow to Donnelley's oldest and best telephone company customer, Illinois Bell Telephone, of the corporate move to New York. It was hoped that the restructuring of directory operations would reassure all the telephone companies that Donnelley intended to give "undivided attention to this most important and major part of our business."[4]

Donnelley's contract with the New York Telephone Company was due to expire on April 1, 1964. With Arnold now in Chicago, the responsibility for managing the negotiation of a new contract fell to the Operating Vice President for the New York region, George Galloway, and to Edward O'Rorke, who was at that time Vice President of the Magazine Publishing Division. Having been both General Sales Manager and General Manager of the Directory Division's New York Region, O'Rorke was well acquainted with the region and with New York Telephone when the negotiations began in 1963. During that important year he took over most of the responsibility for the NYPS operation in New York, so that Galloway could concentrate on making a good showing in local directory sales. In January of 1964, O'Rorke moved over full-time to directory operations, becoming Executive Vice president of the Donnelley Telephone Directory Company. Later, he succeeded Arnold as the head of this company, and Galloway became a regional Vice President.[5]

As the contract talks with New York Telephone progressed, Donnelley worked to strengthen its bargaining position. Two major records management programs were developed in 1963. The first was the conversion of the NYPS records to S.O.U.N.D., a standardized system that laid the groundwork for computerization. Although Donnelley had determined that it would gain little from this conversion, it proceeded with an investment of almost $500,000, largely in order to maintain its prominent position in NYPS. A second program was one that promised to be more rewarding financially—the computerization of the entire records system of the downstate New York operation. This was a project funded and managed jointly with New York Telephone, and it was the first of its kind in the Bell System.

1964: *New contract with New York Telephone becomes effective July 1, 1964 . . . The Beatles break all existing sales records with "She Loves You" and "I Want to Hold Your Hand" . . . California becomes the state with the largest population . . . Michelangelo's "Pieta" is brought to New York for the Vatican exhibit at the World's Fair . . . The U.S. Navy begins Sealab experiments.*

There was also an all-out effort to improve sales performance in 1963. Some six months before the Manhattan Classified was to go to press, O'Rorke brought William L. Johnson to New York from C & P. The rising managerial star from the company's top-performing region, Bill Johnson was named assistant to George Galloway, in charge of sales. In 1933, Clarence Lillyblade had first advanced a coherent vision of directory selling as a profession. But it was Bill Johnson who began, in New York in the mid-1960s, to give that vision concrete reality. By year's end, Manhattan had achieved a 2.4 percent gain in advertising sales, an increase of more than three times that of the previous year. In the first quarter of 1964, the Brooklyn book, which had lost 2 percent the year before, closed with a 3 percent gain. The Staten Island directory posted an 8.9 percent gain, and the canvass in Queens achieved a sales increase of 5 percent.[6]

The new contract with New York Telephone, effective on July 1, 1964, marks a major watershed in the history of Donnelley Directory. O'Rorke and Galloway conducted the final negotiations and succeeded in convincing New York Telephone that Donnelley intended to make the necessary financial commitment and, equally important, that it had the expertise to make, finally, some lasting improvements in the metropolitan operation. Dissatisfied with Donnelley performance during the decade since the previous reforms New York Telephone had reduced its commission for the downstate New York directories from 25 percent to 22.5 percent. It was now raised to 23 percent, but with the agreement that half of this added income would be given back to the operation. For its part, the New York Telephone Company agreed to underwrite a $2.25 million market development program over the following three and one-half years. The contract signaled a recognition by both parties that large expenditures and radical changes were needed.[7]

Grading and Assigning Accounts

Bill Johnson had begun his Donnelley career selling directory advertising in upstate New York before World War II. He was one of the salesmen who returned from the war to find the business transformed and, largely on the basis of that experience, he became convinced that selling the Yellow Pages would be a relatively simple matter for a truly professionalized sales force. The expertise that he brought to New York from the C & P region had developed there over 15 years through the experience of building a sales organization from scratch in a relatively good market area, through interaction with a management team assembled from different regions, through long hours of discussion with his colleagues, and through experimentation, on a small scale, in the C & P region.

One of the most important ideas to come out of this experience was that only about 50 percent to 60 percent of all business telephone accounts were worth the effort of regular solicitation for advertising. Moreover, even among these, there were appreciable differences in the level of contact required. Johnson therefore proposd to New York Telephone early on under the new contract that Donnelley undertake a program of market appraisal to investigate and grade accounts in the downstate area according to their sales potential.[8]

The grading of accounts was far from a new concept within Donnelley. Indeed, it first began when the company stopped turning out brand-new prospect cards for every canvass, so that the information that salesmen collected could be used again. Traditionally, however, grading had been done almost exclusively on the basis of the dollar value of accounts. Moreover, while it was often true that more advanced Account Executives handled the so-called major accounts, it was also not uncommon for prospect cards to be distributed to sales representatives according to the principle that everyone should have his share of good prospects and bad. In contrast, the system that was developed in New York in the 1960s used not just dollar value, but also activity and even growth potential, to grade accounts. In addition, it created a much more elaborate hierarchy of sales positions, so that a person's skill and experience could be matched to accounts that would provide an appropriate level of challenge and opportunity.[9]

The decision to give up the attempt to call or visit every account was a major departure for the telephone industry, and it was not an easy one for telephone companies to accept. Yet it was a change that promised to revitalize Donnelley's sales performance as no other innovation had done before. Inactive accounts—"the carryover market"—were continually graded downward from year to year, many to the point where no regular contact was made, and the advertising was simply continued on a " 'til forbid" basis. As the handling of such accounts had formerly been the primary occupation of the telephone sales departments, these were now able to take on the responsibility and opportunity of more promising accounts that did not require a premise sales call. "We shall concentrate upon selected quality coverage of the market as against mass quantity coverage," Ham Mitchell explained to the Board:

> This will enable us to handle by telephone solicitation, industry groups which are less interested in Yellow Page advertising and concentrate our premise sales efforts on more susceptible areas of the market. Increased premise effort in the better industry headings should improve sales at practically no increase in cost.[10]

Once a more refined system of account assignments had been developed, it was possible to institute a more complex program of compensation, one that offered greater incentives. One of the first steps taken in the New York operation was to reduce the number of sales representatives and to increase substantially the pay of those that remained. Eventually, what evolved was a compensation plan based not strictly on commission, as it always had been, but involving a base salary plus commission. For the first time, Donnelley could afford to pay its sales people well, because the structure of the organization promoted high performance at all levels. This new situation produced not only immediate improvements in sales results, but also a dramatic drop in the rate of employee turnover, from highs of 70 percent and more per year to lows of 10 percent and even 8 percent. As the sales force stabilized and the assignment of accounts became more systematic, it was possible to establish greater continuity of relationships between sales people and their customers. In short, there were greater earnings, greater security, better service to advertisers, increased revenues for the telephone companies, and greater profits for Donnelley. These characteristics became the hallmark of the professionalized sales organization.[11]

New Ventures and Self Examination

The team of Johnson and Galloway in New York, with O'Rorke at the head of the Directory Company, remained in place until 1968. The success of the programs that they were developing in New York and slowly spreading to the other regions began to make a significant change in Donnelley's outlook. The long-felt desire to play a leadership role in the directory industry was transformed into a conviction that Donnelley was, indeed, the leader in terms of professionalization and performance. This conviction, in turn, sparked an interest in expanding the company's field of operation. In 1965, an agreement was struck with the British Thomson Organization, whereby Donnelley would act as consultant in taking over the sale of advertising in, and compilation of, classified and alphabetical directories in

---

1969: The Donnelley-Directory Record *circulates within and without the company, published in a magazine format . . . The longest dock strike in U.S. history ends after 57 days . . . Richard M. Nixon becomes the 37th President of the United States . . . Neil Armstrong is the first man on the moon . . . The AngloFrench supersonic aircraft, the Concorde, makes it first test flight . . . Warren Earl Burger becomes Chief Justice of the Supreme Court.*

Great Britain. Donnelley and Thomson also agreed to pursue opportunities to obtain directory business in other parts of the world, and discussions soon began in Greece, Italy, Canada, and Australia. In addition, Donnelley began to negotiate on its own for the acquisition of the International Yellow Pages.

In 1966, the company turned its attention to the problem of expansion in the domestic market, deciding to take active steps to expand its shape in the industry. By the beginning of 1969, Donnelley was making new business presentations around the county to a number of companies, both Bell and independent. In addition, its newest division, Directory International, was in the process of starting up a new publication for the Canadian and U.S. market, *The National Buyer's Guide,* a reference for commercial and industrial buyers conceived as an extension of the International Yellow Pages.[12]

All of these new ventures were initiated in the context of changes within the organization and of a growing sense of the need for direction. In 1966, the Telephone Directory Company returned to divisional status within Reuben H. Donnelley, with Ed O'Rorke remaining as its head. He initiated a number of projects that were clearly aimed at long-range results and hired Basic Systems (which later became Xerox Learning Systems) as consultants to study directory selling techniques as a first step toward revising and restructuring Donnelley's sales training programs. Another consulting firm, Smyth & Murphy, helped to develop further refinements in sales compensation. In addition, O'Rorke started an internal operations research project to determine the future impact of changing technology on our product. During 1967, the impulse that motivated these programs was formalized in a five-year plan, which included an individual plan for each region and an overall plan for the Division as a whole. By the first quarter of 1968, the major components of that plan had already been set in motion. Bill Johnson was sent down as Vice President to Penn/Delaware, so that the last remaining trouble-spot would be brought up to current Donnelley standards. The study on selling techniques culminated in "Yellow Pages Selling Skills," an innovative training program introduced companywide and shared with the Bell System.

Another study, undertaken by Cresap, McCormick, and Paget in 1967, recommended integrating the regional NYPS operations into a single functional unit. A second Cresap project, the following year, led to a similar plan for unifying the entire directory operation. The basic thrust of both reports was the same. In order to achieve continued improvements in sales results, or to position itself for growth or expansion into new markets, the Donnelley Directory Division needed to pull itself together into a unified and uniformly professionalized sales organization. In almost every area—training, marketing, and sales support—there was wasteful duplication in the four separate regions. The quality of regional materials varied widely, in part because there was no mechanism for sharing improvements among the regions. Moreover, even when new ideas were shared, there was often resistance to adopting them from regional hierarchies long accustomed to their own ways of doing things.[13]

Cresap's recommendations and O'Rorke's determination to implement them were of the greatest significance for the future of the Donnelley Directory Division. Ultimately, the new unification would be far more thoroughgoing than that of the Harrington era, moving beyond the imposition of common standards upon the regional organizations by taking away from them key functions such as training and the design of promotional and sales support materials.[14]

A Changing Environment

The self analysis that occurred within Donnelley in the late 1960s was driven in part by changes within the Bell System. For many years AT&T had made major contributions to the directory industry by establishing standards and by promoting usage through advertising. Beginning in the late 1950s, however, it began to play a new role in what had always been a very sectionalized, fragmented corporate system. The most obvious example of this was the establishment in 1957 of a system-wide task force, in which Donnelley was invited to participate, to standardize the selling of national advertising. This group produced NYPS in 1960. In addition, AT&T began to pull together the internally run directory operations of the Bell System, creating task forces, study groups, and management conferences designed to improve overall performance.[15]

Donnelley shared its growing expertise and its new sales training and support materials with the Bell companies, but it became increasingly clear that professionalism and success would not ensure forever a secure place within the system. In 1968, Donnelley's business with New York Telephone in the western area, centered in Buffalo, was arbitrarily taken away and given to a competitor, L. M. Berry. New York Telephone assured Donnelley that there was no complaint about performance. The explanation for this action was simply that it "would establish Berry as a more important supplier in the future, and give the New York Telephone Company the choice of another qualified directory sales agent." The message was clear: while Donnelley was, without dispute, a leader in the directory industry, it was still subservient to the telephone system on which the industry depended.

PRESIDENTS OF THE
REUBEN H. DONNELLEY CORPORATION

Reuben H. Donnelley
1917-1927

PRESIDENTS OF THE
REUBEN H. DONNELLEY CORPORATION

George W. Overton
1929-1942

Raymond M. Gunnison
1942-1951

David L. Harrington
1951-1956

Curtiss E. Frank
1956-1961

"Duke" Drake Takes Over

By the end of 1968 Ham Mitchell had become President of D&B, and Harrington ("Duke") Drake had succeeded him as president of Reuben H. Donnelley. Drake was supportive of the kinds of changes that were under way in the Directory Division and understood the need to make substantial investments to upgrade the sales effort. His support was tested early, when he was confronted with, and endorsed, large unbudgeted expenses in Penn/Delaware that came from Bill Johnson's first act in the region—moving the entire operation out of its rather shabby offices into one of the newest buildings in Philadelphia.[16]

At the same time, Drake gave O'Rorke the freedom that he needed to take radical measures on a larger scale. His first move toward centralization was the creation of a unified support staff for NYPS sales in the four regions. The second was the establishment of a Directory Operations Group as an "umbrella" organization charged with providing marketing and sales support wherever it was needed in the organization. A third step was the creation of the Plans Council, a group of second-line managers from all over the Directory Division, meeting monthly for open-ended discussion of both short-range and long-range concerns. In reality, the plans Council was both a forum within which companywide issues could be discussed and regional barriers broken down, and a vehicle by which common standards could be established throughout the organization.

All of these three key steps were taken in 1969. In addition, in the fall of that year, a new divisional publication was launched—*The Donnelley-Directory Record.* With a high-quality, magazine-style format, *The Record* was designed to serve a dual purpose. To the outside world, it touted Donnelley's professionalism and kept people in the industry well informed of every innovation and improvement. Within, it served as the voice of the Directory Operations Group, presenting innovations in ways that would promote understanding and generate enthusiasm and support in the ranks.

In 1970, Bill Johnson returned to New York as General Manager of the Directory Division, assuming the major responsibility for implementing O'Rorke's plans for a centralized organization as well as his own vision of a truly professionalized directory sales operation. In failing health, O'Rorke retired at the end of 1971, "You should be proud," he told a farewell party in Chicago, "to work for the most professional sales organization in the country." To a great extent, O'Rorke was responsible for bringing the organization to that point and, equally, for setting in motion the changes that would carry it to an even higher level of professionalism in the future.[17]

Reorganization was effected in a variety of ways. Most visible was the constant stream of new materials flowing out of the Directory

Operations Group. These included marketing data and analyses, specialized presentation materials, streamlined sales support packages, and a firm set of guidelines for the design and production of all sales promotion items. Behind the scenes, the adoption and effective use of such materials was facilitated by management policies designed to create a sales support organization with a professionalism to complement that of the sales staff. Changing the label on this function from "non-sales" to "sales support" was a first step in this direction, but more important was the reversal of a long-standing policy of spending as little as possible on this work. Many policies of long standing, at all levels of management, had to be changed as the reforms that had been initiated in New York beginning in 1964 were pushed out through corporate headquarters into the regional operations.[18]

In 1971 and 1972, the idea of a Plans Council was expanded into a Management Council and, for lower-level managers, a Production Council and a Sales Council. Quarterly meetings of these councils helped to create a corporate culture supportive of the high level of integration that was the ultimate goal. Similarly, the creation of a centralized training program for new employees was a way to foster loyalties to Donnelley Directory as a whole that would take precedence over—or at least equal—those that would inevitably develop in any regional office.

By the mid-1970s, the creation of the professionalized sales organization was substantially complete, and the transformation was strongly reflected in Donnelley's performance, as Figure 4 shows. In the 12 years

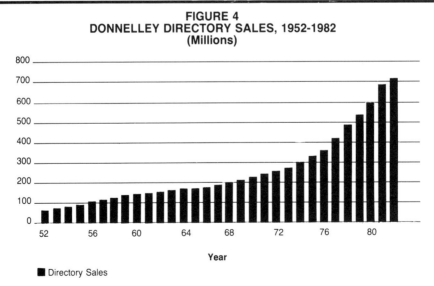

FIGURE 4
DONNELLEY DIRECTORY SALES, 1952-1982
(Millions)

■ Directory Sales

Source: For 1934-1961, see Figure 3. Figures for 1962-1972 compiled from Annual Reports, Board Minutes, Series 2, Vols. III-XII. Figures for 1972-1982 were compiled by Joe Constantino of Donnelley.

PRESIDENTS OF THE
REUBEN H. DONNELLEY CORPORATION

Hamilton B. Mitchell
1961-1968

Harrington E. Drake, Jr.
1968-1972

Joseph W. Hight
1972-1976

William L. Johnson
1976-1977

PRESIDENTS OF THE
REUBEN H. DONNELLEY CORPORATION

James E. Rutter
1977-1982

Richard B. Swank
1982-1984

William Bak
Donnelley Information Publishing
1984-

Kenneth O. Johnson
Donnelley Directory
1984-

from 1956 to 1968, sales revenues had risen from $100 million to $200 million. In the succeeding 12 years, they rose to $600 million, on the way to even higher levels in the 1980s. Undoubtedly these gains were largely the product of rate increases, which continued throughout this period of high inflation. But, in contrast to earlier years, when it had been difficult to produce consistent results to match rate increases, Donnelley now posted solid sales gains to augment the general upward trend in rates.

Now more than ever, Donnelley could believe that there was real value added by its sales effort. Not only were its Yellow pages salesmen more effective, but also there were improvements in the product that made it more saleable. One of Donnelley's most notable contributions was the split of the 2,600-page Chicago classified directory into two volumes, the Buyers' Guide, a traditional Yellow Pages for consumers, and the Commercial and Industrial Directory, a more specialized directory that was not delivered to every telephone subscriber, but only to businesses. Three years of work went into the preparations for this change, but it paid off in substantial savings in cost and increased usage of the more convenient "B" and "C" directories.[19]

In the 1970s, Donnelley people began to talk about changing from a sales organization to a marketing organization as newly scoped directories, second-color red, coupons, and innovative market rate plans vied for attention in *The Record*. A concept of marketing had been articulated in 1962 by Don Arnold's marketing coordinator, who described it as:

> . . . the management of many interdependent activities. Through *research* and *analysis* (of market, product, users and buyers, sales, personnel), it must develop a program (involving product, promotion, training, sales selection, management and objectives) and then put it into action (with proper organization, coordination and timing) to get results: sales, profits, leadership.

It had not been enough, however, simply to understand how marketing should work and its potential value. The implementation of this concept had to wait for the creation of a sales organization capable of performing all of the necessary tasks. It is a kind of tribute to the achievements of Johnson and O'Rorke that they were so soon taken for granted.[20]

A New D&B

"Duke" Drake, who had presided over the process of centralization, left Donnelley to assume the Presidency of D&B at the end of 1972 and was succeeded by Joseph W. Hight. Hight had made a switch in the opposite direction—from D&B to Donnelley—earlier in the year. This move marked the opening of new opportunities for executives to move in either direction. In addition, the selection of Hight as Donnelley President signaled the beginning of changes in the relationship between the two companies toward more interaction and more active leadership by D&B. Soon it was announced within Donnelley that a recognition was planned as a means of effecting these changes.[21]

Drake's vision was to unify the loosely associated companies within D&B, much as Donnelley had been unified, and to reshape them into a more smoothly functioning whole. In order to be capable of outstanding performance, D&B would have to meet three major objectives: In the first place, it must become more responsive to current needs of customers. Secondly, it must anticipate these customers' future needs. And finally, it must develop altogether new customers.[22]

By January of 1976 the D&B reorganization was complete. As a result, Donnelley's Marketing Division became a separate entity—Donnelley Marketing—joined together with other D&B marketing services under a single executive vice president. Magazine Publishing was combined with various D&B publishing activites into Dun-Donnelley Publishing and organized, also under an executive vice president, into a division representing communications services. Directory remained part of an entity called Reuben H. Donnelley that also included a Transportation, Guides and Services Division producing the *Official Airline Guide* and the several *Travel Age* magazines.

This new organization made it possible for Donnelley to do away with its large corporate structure and staff, as D&B took over most of the functions they had served. D&B provided other services as well, particularly in the area of human resources, and Donnelley people gained from being able to participate in D&B's employee-benefit programs. Most important in the long run, the reorganization meant that senior management in all the D&B companies operated in a structure demanding interchange and cooperation. Within this framework of mutual support, they could undertake such things as budgeting, forecasting, and strategic planning on a scale that had been impossible before.[23]

In the process of these changes, Joseph Hight became D&B Executive Vice President in charge of Reuben H. Donnelley, and William

---

1976: Dun-Donnelley Publishing *created . . . The United States celebrates the 200th Anniversary of its independence . . . Woodward and Bernstein publish* The Final Days, *about Richard Nixon's last days in the White House . . . Jimmy Carter and Walter Mondale are elected President and Vice President . . . The film* Rocky, *starring Sylvester Stallone, wins the Academy Award for best picture . . . Pioneer 10 travels through Saturn's rings and heads toward a 1987 examination of Pluto.*

L. Johnson became Reuben H. Donnelley President. Within a year, Johnson was Chairman of the board, and at the end of 1977 he retired, feeling that he had accomplished all that he had set out to do. [24]

VII

Toward the Second Century

(1978-1986)

In the mid-1970s, the world of classified directory publishing was changing in subtle but significant ways. Not least important was the fact that AT&T was continuing to strengthen its presence in this area of the Bell System. Interviewed in 1979 by the *Donnelley-Directory Record*, the head of AT&T's directory operation, Edward Hancharik, clearly articulated the new policy:

> *The Record:* Are you changing your posture here at AT&T head-quarters?
>
> *Ed Hancharik:* Yes, there is a change. We'll be taking a more directive role! We'll be taking a stronger Systems posture. For example: we'll be recommending a similar Business-to-Business cover for all business directories. We'll insist that the Bell Companies use the same cover design. On the important issues, we'll be a little more directive than we've been; a little more forceful than we've been—because there's a need to be more uniform—not to reinvent the wheel.[1]

At the same time, however, AT&T was beginning to confront forces that called into question the propriety of its playing such a role. For example, in 1974 an antitrust suit had been brought against NYPS as a cartel, and a year later that organization had been restructured as the National Yellow Pages Service Association (NYPSA), an independent association open to all Yellow Pages publishers. Having come somewhat recently to the recognition of the value and potential value of the directory business, AT&T was not to be stopped in its movement toward greater control over Yellow Pages within the Bell System. Yet a signal had gone up warning that some changes in the industry might come from the direction of the Justice Department.[2]

For its part, Donnelley was striving to maintain a position of leadership in the industry and to find new areas of growth. The centralization and professionalization of the previous decade had, for all practical purposes, eradicated the differences in sales capabilities among the regions. At the same time, the centralization of the NYPS organization had transformed it into a distinct entity and a major contributor of revenue—almost a "region" in its own right. Having brought these four units up to an even, high level of performance, Donnelley continued to seek growth within the constraints of its relationship to the Bell System.

Strategic Planning

The corporate marketing staff played an important role in this effort. The so-called marketing innovations—newly scoped directories, coupons, second-color red, community sections ("green pages")—were highly visible contributions to continuing revenue gains in Donnelley's relatively stable, nongrowth market areas. Concurrently, in its quest for new business, the company turned to a vigorous developmental program aimed at independent telephone companies. Each region appointed a new manager of directory development with full-time responsibility for this effort. The list of Donnelley's independent telephone company clients in Illinois and Pennsylvania grew steadily after 1975, and a nearly moribund sales office in Scranton, Pennsylvania, was given new life as a publishing facility to serve those in the East. In 1979, contracts with Central Telephone & Utilities Corporation (CENTEL) for directories in North Carolina as well as Virginia, and with the Winter Park Telephone Company for the directory of Winter Park, Florida, took Donnelley into new geographic areas for the first time since the establishment of C & P region 30 years before. With its strong rate of growth, reflected in a rapidly rising number of telephones, Winter Park, in particular, was the kind of area that Donnelley sought.[3]

By 1979, however, the directory organization began to address the problem of continued growth in new ways. James E. Rutter was President of Reuben H. Donnelley at this time, having succeeded Bill Johnson two years before. Rutter had come from D&B, with Hight, in 1972, first as Vice President and later as Senior Vice President in charge of three divisions—Transportation Guides & Services, Travel Magazines, and Teleflora. As President, he inherited what was probably the best sales and marketing organization in the directory industry at the time. In addition, he was the beneficiary of the energy and resources created by the recent reorganization of D&B and of the vital interest that "Duke" Drake, as Chief Executive Officer of D&B, took in the future of Donnelley. With Drake's backing, Rutter brought to the directory organization a concept of strategic planning capable of lifting it from its plateau of established excellence to a new position from which it would be able to find and take advantage of opportunities for growth.

The first step in translating that concept into action was the assembling of a management team open to strategic thinking. Donnelley's directory organization was put under the joint leadership of Richard B. Swank, Senior Vice President responsible for the overall direction of the four regions, and Burton A. Ford, Senior Vice President responsible for technical areas such as publishing, production mechanization, and computerization. Swank's career at Donnelley had begun in New York in the mid-1960s and included a major role in the Directory Operations Group in 1969. In the mid-1970s, he headed the company's European operations and became involved in Thomson Yellow Pages as a director, and on returning from England he had become Vice President and General Manager of the Penn/Delaware region. Ford had joined Donnelley's C & P region in its early years and had been part of the circle of colleagues around Bill Johnson who had helped envision the policies leading to a more professionalized sales operation. Subsequently, he had risen in management of the Directory Division, and he was Swank's immediate predecessor as Vice President of Penn/Delaware, moving to become Vice President of the New York region after 1974.

Another important member of the team was LaRue G. ("Buck") Buchanan. Buchanan had started with Donnelley as a salesman in Albany in 1946 and rose to Area Manager in Buffalo before moving to downstate New York, where he was the regional General Sales Manager and later General Manager of NYPS. He had also held a staff position at Donnelley headquarters, and, in 1969, he was tapped by Ed O'Rorke to organize and lead the Directory Operations Group as Vice President and General Manager of Directory Operations Services. In the late 1970s, "Buck" Buchanan remained closely involved in implementing the company's strategic plans, as Vice President of Marketing.

1979: *Project GO and the Operations Task Force result in increased productivity and efficiency. . . New contracts for directories take Donnelley into new market areas for the first time in 30 years. . . Tom Wolfe publishes* The Right Stuff, *about the training and private lives of the seven original astronauts. . . Pope John Paul II visits five American cities . . . Mother Teresa of India is awarded the Nobel Peace Prize . . . Jane M. Byrne is the first woman to be elected Mayor of Chicago.*

The 1980's: *After divestiture and Project P, the Reuben H. Donnelley Company— now two entities, Donnelley Directory and Donnelley Information Publishing, charts a new course into its second century.*

In 1979 and 1980, two new faces appeared at Donnelley head-quarters, William Bak and Kenneth O. Johnson. Within a few years, fol-lowing a move by Burt Ford to D&B and the retirement of "Buck" Buchanan, these two men would join Dick Swank in the inner circle of Donnelley's decision-makers. Bill Bak, like Buchanan, had started out in sales in upstate New York and had advanced to Area Manager in Buffalo. But he was the one who had to close down that office when the area was given to Donnelley's competitor, L. M. Berry, in 1968. After this, he moved to the Downstate operation, and after several years as a sales manager, took a staff position as assistant to Bill Johnson, who was then Senior Vice President. Sub-sequently, Bak moved out to Chicago, and he had advanced to Assistant Vice President in the Illinois/Cincinnati region when he was called back to New York in 1979 to become Assistant Vice President for Sales Planning.

Ken Johnson came to Donnelley Directory headquarters in 1980 from Penn/Delaware, where he had followed Dick Swank as regional Vice President. Johnson had begun his association with the Yellow Pages as a Donnelley customer, the owner of a small business in Chicago. He joined the sales force there in 1958 and by 1970 advanced to General Manager for NYPS in Illinois/Cincinnati. In 1971, he moved to the New York region and six years later to Penn/Delaware, where he remained until called upon to lead a corporate task force on cost control.

Under "Buck" Buchanan, the role of marketing expanded beyond increasing revenues in established markets into finding new sources of rev-enue. It was this impulse that produced *New Connections* and the *Health Care Industry Directory*. Under Ford, Donnelley's publication facilities made many advances, particularly in a joint program with Illinois Bell to develop MIDAS (Mechanized Illinois Bell/Donnelley Advertising System), a computerized system integrating order processing, compilation, and com-position. By 1982, Donnelley's Terre Haute publication center would be not only the largest but also one of the most technologically advanced in the nation. At the same time, the publishing operation in Scranton was setting its own records for rapid growth and improvement, keeping pace with the expansion of Donnelley's growing business with independent telephone companies.

These marketing and publishing advances placed the company in a stronger position within the Bell System, and, in general, Donnelley maintained a high profile in this period in keeping with its self-image as the industry's leader. In 1977, for example, it sponsored a marketing con-ference, attended by executives from all of its major telephone company clients, for the purpose of presenting Donnelley's "marketing philosophy and new approaches being used to serve advertisers and users." In a similar spirit, the company actively disseminated its most up-to-date training materials within the industry. In 1980, however, a significant step was taken outside the system, with the decision to launch competing directories in Great Britain, after Donnelley and Thomson lost their contract for the official Yellow Pages. Still remaining a loyal "vendor" in the U.S., Donnelley seized this opportunity to find out—and to show others as well—what it could do in a competitive situation, when and if the need arose.[4]

Project GO and the Operations Task Force

A new project was started in January 1979 that addressed the issues of growth and industry leadership in a fundamental way. Led by Bill Bak, Project GO ("Growth Opportunities") began with a study, made jointly by Donnelley and McKinsey management consultants of the entire directory sales operation, from management in the central office to sales out in the field. A number of specific proposals came out of this study, but the main thrust of the recommendations was that further improvements in sales performance could be achieved primarily by raising the level of professionalization in management. Donnelley could benefit in particular, the report argued, from improved management of information, especially from a more rigorous application of available data to the very complex problems of sales quotas and compensation. Within its substantially mature market areas, the company needed to find new ways to motivate sales people to perform better than average if its revenues were to continue to grow.[5]

Project GO gave new meaning to Donnelley's long-established image as a "people company." At the same time, it carried the technological revolution begun in the early 1960s to an entirely new level. With systems such as DSRS, ASSIST, and the Sales Information Services for mini-computers, computerization brought to the sales side of the business the same kind of support that had earlier been given to production—technological support intended to help people perform better.[6]

With Project GO in its implementation phase, a new team, the Operations Task Force, was created to address the problem of growth not by increasing revenues but by cutting costs. Under its chairman, Ken Johnson, the Operations Task Force scrutinized procedures and costs in every area of the company. Their approach was to define and analyze functional units that cut across the boundaries of geographic regions. Having done this, they could determine a single "best" method of performing each necessary operation, so that that method could be adopted by like units companywide.[7]

Project GO and the Operations Task Force were successful attempts to create growth through greater productivity and increased efficiency. They carried the process of change begun in the early 1960s to its conclusion. The professionalization of the sales force started with an effort to analyze the directory market more precisely than had been done before, to assign accounts more appropriately according to experience and capability, to provide a higher level of sales support, and to compensate more fairly on the basis of productivity. The objectives of Project GO were essentially the same, but it was then possible, with the aid of computer technology and the advantage of the many changes that had accrued over fifteen years, to accomplish these at a much higher level of complexity, matching of the many changes that had accrued over 15 years, to accomplish these at a much higher level of complexity, matching that of the problems involved. Similarly, the Operations Task Force achieved a degree of unification that would not have been possible a decade before. The motivating vision of making "the best practice . . . the norm at Donnelley" was shared by both generations of reformers—those of the 1960s and early 1970s, led by O'Rorke and Bill Johnson, and those rising with Dick Swank, who took over the reins as President of Donnelley in 1982. When Swank became president, however, AT&T's divestiture case was already under way. The changes that Donnelley was soon to experience would take this 96-year-old company off in a wholly new direction, one that demanded a vision and a self-image that would have been unthinkable a decade before.[8]

After Divestiture: Project P

In order to prepare for whatever might come out of divestiture, Swank assembled another project team, "Project P" (for Proprietary Planning). Although it was clear early on that there would be independent Bell companies when the case was finally concluded, it was not until August 1983 that the planning group knew whether these companies, or AT&T, would control the directory business. A viable plan for the future had to include alternate strategies for both possible outcomes.[9]

The capacity of Donnelley's leadership to meet this challenge was greatly enhanced by the support they received from D&B. Since 1976, annual D&B management meetings had provided a forum that encouraged strategic planning. At the same time, the combined resources of the D&B companies made it possible to complete strategies that might require considerable financial backing to succeed. There was also strength to be gained from D&B's resources and expertise in information technology.[10]

Donnelley's position was further strengthened by its own experience and expertise. The establishment of competing directories in England provided many valuable lessons, the most important of which was undoubtedly that it was possible to compete against the "official" Yellow Pages. Moreover, a momentum had been building up within Donnelley since the late 1970s—a force for expansion fed by the almost continuous series of operational improvements and innovations and by the ever rising levels of performance that these produced. Within the constraints of the old Bell system, this force was diverted into noncompetitive channels. Released by the court decision of August 1983 that gave the regional Bell companies control over their own directory operations, its momentum catapulted Donnelley into a whole new set of situations and relationships, each filled with risks and opportunities that never existed in predivestiture days.

The breakup of the Bell System became effective January 1, 1984. By the end of the first quarter of 1985 Donnelley had negotiated a partnership with Ameritech (AM-DON) in the Midwest and one with the independent United Telephone Company (UNI-DON) in the South. It had acquired the National Directory Company of California, which had been the largest directory publisher outside of the Bell System, and was setting up operations in Houston, Tulsa, and Oklahoma City. By June 1985, San Antonio and Daytona Beach had also been added to the list of Donnelley's directory operations. Soon after, the company announced that it lost its contract for the "official" Yellow Pages in its old Penn/Delaware region and that it would, after 1986, publish its own directories there, in competition with Bell Atlantic. Thus, in short order, the company had forged a new, stronger working relationship with its oldest customer and had entered vigorously into competition in other areas, particularly in the kinds of high-growth market areas it had so long been denied.

Yet Reuben H. Donnelley was no longer even a single company. It had been transformed into two new entities—Donnelley Directory, and Donnelley Information Publishing. The former was placed under the direction of Ken Johnson, who, since finishing his work with the Operations Task Force, had been Vice President for the Mid-Atlantic region; the latter under Bill Bak, Senior Vice President in the Northeast region since the conclusion of Project GO. Both Johnson and Bak had participated in Project P. Swank retained overall control as the D&B Executive Vice President responsible for the two directory companies.

These men, who had played leading roles in shaping a strategy to carry the organization into its second century, were now charged with the responsibility for implementing that strategy. Donnelley Directory was structured to function as sales agent within contractual relationships such as the AM-DON and UNI-DON partnerships, and Donnelley Information Publishing was set up to pursue its own course as an independent directory publisher in whatever areas might offer the best opportunities.[11]

Thus, by the start of its 100th year, the Donnelley directory organization had come full circle to the entrepreneurism of its founder—both in sales and in publishing. On May 15, 1986, the company celebrates the day that Reuben H. Donnelley produced his first classified telephone directory, the prototypes of our Yellow Pages. If "R.H." himself could return to share in that celebration, he would find a company wildly altered in outward form, yet in spirit one that he would undoubtedly recognize as his own.

NOTES TO CHAPTER I

1. On the appearance of Chicago in the 1840s, Harriet Martineau, 1843, quoted in Harold M. Mayer and Richard C. Wade, *Chicago: Growth of a Metropolis* (Chicago: University of Chicago Press, 1969), 22. "The Mushroom Metropolis," quotation from the St. Louis *Globe Democrat*, n.d., dateline August 6 [1904], in "Historical Information File," organized by year, maintained in the corporate archives of Donnelley Directory/ Donnelley Information Publishing in the Pierce Business Archives, Spring Valley, New York (hereafter cited as Hist. Info. File).

2. Chicago's population growth from 1864 to 1929 is calculated from decadal rates given in Chicago Municipal Reference Department, comp., *Historical Information About Chicago* (Chicago, 1975), 3. According to census data, the Northeast Region was the most populous through 1860, and the South moved ahead of the North Central Region after 1930: c.f., U.S. Bureau of the Census, *Historical Statistics of the United States— Colonial Times to 1970, Bicentennial Edition, Part I* (Washington, D.C., 1975), Series A, 172-194, 22-23. Between 1880 and 1890, the number of manufacturing establishments in Chicago grew by 184%, the amount of capital invested in manufacturing by 422%, the gross value of manufactures by 167%, and the value added by manufacturing by 264%. In every category of growth, Chicago far exceeded both New York and Philadelphia, the two leading manufacturing cities in this period: statistics calculated from Bessie Louise Pierce, *A History of Chicago, Volume III, The Rise of a Modern City, 1871-1893* (Chicago, 1957), Appendix Table, "Leading Cities in Manufacturing, 1880, 1890," 533.

3. This paragraph is based primarily on Mayer and Wade, *Chicago*, 24-28, 35-36, 42-44; the quotation is from p. 28. Statistics on wheat and lumber are calculated from Bessie Louise Pierce, *A History of Chicago, Volume II, From Town to City, 1848-1871* (Chicago: University of Chicago Press, 1940), Appendix, 495-496.

4. For the quotations in this paragraph, Mayer and Wade, *Chicago*, 48, 44. Figures for merchandise calculated from Pierce, *From Town to City*, Appendix, 495-498.

5. Gaylord Donnelley, "Donnelley History, The Beginning: 1864-1874," *The Donnelley Printer* (Spring, 1965), 39-42.

6. Gaylord Donnelley, "The Beginning," 42-44; Anon., "The Story of the Predecessor of the Reuben H. Donnelley Corporation" (August, 1933), in the folder "Letterheads" (maintained with Hist. Info. File), 1; and "Chronological Development of R. R. Donnelley & Sons Company and The Reuben H. Donnelley Corporation," *Lakeside Press Magazine* (August, 1933), 184.

7. On city directories, Peter R. Knights, "City Directories as Aids to Ante-Bellum Urban Studies: A Research Note," *Historical Methods Newsletter*, 2:4 (1969), 4-5; and Dorothea N. Spear, comp., *Bibliography of American Directories Through 1860* (Worcester, Mass.: American Antiquarian Society, 1961).

8. "The Story of the Predecessors of the Reuben H. Donnelley Corporation," 1-2; "Chronological Development of R. R. Donnelley & Sons Company and The Reuben H. Donnelley Corporation," in *Lakeside Press Magazine* (August, 1933), 184-185.

9. Gaylord Donnelley, "A Decade of Reorganization, 1874–1883," *The Donnelley Printer* (Summer, 1965), 30-31.

10. Ibid., 32-33; and "Donnelley History," passim.

11. On attendance at the old University of Chicago and his rise through the canvassing department of the Chicago Directory Co., his obituary, prepared for the Chicago *Daily News* (Hist. Info. File, 1929). On attendance at "Bryant's Business College," Gaylord Donnelley, "Decade of Reorganization," 32. For the full name, Bessie Louise Pierce, *A History of Chicago, Vol. III, The Rise of a Modern City* (Chicago: University of Chicago Press, 1957), 395.

12. "R. R. Donnelley & Sons, Publishers," appears on the title page of this directory. The Chicago Telephone Company held a virtual monopoly in Chicago. This company was created in 1881 by the merger of the Bell Telephone Company and the American District Telegraph Company, both of which had been providing phone service in Chicago since June, 1878.

13. *Chicago Telephone Directory*, May 15, 1886 (Chicago: R. R. Donnelley & Sons, 1886), 4.

14. The description contained in this paragraph and the next is based on examination of the two directories, both of which are in the possession of Donnelley Directory/Donnelley Information Publishing, at their record storage facility in Chicago.

15. This claim was made in the biographical sketch widely published in 1920, at the time of his election to President of the Associated Advertising Clubs of the World. Chicago *Commerce*, March 20, 1920; and *Associated Advertising*, April, 1920. Both are in Hist. Info. File (1920).

NOTES TO CHAPTER II

1. Gaylord Donnelley, "A Century Draws to a Close, 1893-1899," *The Donnelley Printer* (Fall, 1965), 34; and H. P. Zimmerman, "Donnelley and the Telephone Company, Part I: 1886–1906" (Unpublished MSS, December, 1954, maintained in Hist. Info. File), 9.

2. These quotations are from newspaper clippings from 1903, supplied to Donnelley by the Argus Press Clipping Bureau in New York and maintained without identification in the Hist. Info. File (1903).

3. Quotations are from newpaper clippings announcing the appearance of the business directory of 1903 (Hist. Info. File, 1904) and from a letter from the Chicago Directory Company to its business customers, December 16, 1905 (Hist. Info. File, 1905). On the appearance of the 1887 directory, Evert F. Nelson letter to David G. Allen (October 29, 1985), cited hereafter as Nelson Letter.

4. An interview of H. H. McCauley by E. L. Storey, dated September 9, 1939 (publication unknown) in Hist. Info. File (pre-1900); and clippings, ibid. (1903-1906).

5. The form letter soliciting advertising for this directory from businesses outside of Chicago is preserved in Hist. Info. File (1904).

6. Unidentified news clipping in Hist. Info. File (1905).

7. In Hist. Info. File (1903).

8. The Chicago *Daily News,* n.d., Hist. Info. File (1903).

9. The information on Mrs. Donnelley is from an obituary, printed in *The Lakeside Press* (December, 1918), n.p.; and from Donnelley Interview.

10. Chicago *Tribune,* June 1, 1901; and *Chicago Journal,* January 3, 1903, in Hist. Info. File for respective dates. In 1903, Newell C. Knight was police Chief of Evanston.

11. On the telephone company policy regarding display advertising, c.f. A. H. Heldt, "Historical Data," *The Donnelley Advertiser,* 1:3 (1936), 3; and a contract of May 7, 1891, reproduced in Zimmerman, I, 10. Interviewed in 1939, H. H. McCauley, a 40-year veteran of Donnelley directory work, remembered that, of the three main publications of the Chicago Directory Company at the turn of the century (the city directory, *The Blue Book,* and the classified telephone directory), the telephone book was "the least important . . . a mere infant." In Hist. Info. File (pre-1900).

12. Herbert N. Casson, *The History of the Telephone* (Chicago: A. C. McClurg & Co., 1910) 168-169, 178-181. By contrast, England resisted the message rate for many years, and its phone network grew much more slowly: Charles R. Perry, "The British Experience, 1876–1912: The Impact of the Telephone During the Years of Delay," in Ithiel de Sola Pool, ed., *The Social Impact of the Telephone* (Cambridge, Mass.: The MIT Press, 1977), Appendix 2, "Charging Policy," 91-92. The national telephone statistics are from U.S. Bureau of the Census, *Historical Statistics*, Part II, Series R 1-12, 783-784. The Chicago statistics are computed by the author from data given by John H. Keiser, *Building for the Centuries: Illinois, 1865-1898, The Sesquicentennial History of Illinois*, Volume IV (Chicago: University of Illinois Press, 1977), 194.

13. H. P. Zimmerman, "Donnelley and the Telephone Company, Part II: 1906–1916" (unpublished MSS, 1955), Supplement, 10. These contracts were actually with Bell Telephone Company of Buffalo, for Buffalo and Rochester, and with the Hudson River Telephone Company, for Albany and Troy, but these companies were controlled by New York Telephone in 1906 and were taken over completely about 1910.

14. Ibid., 1-5A. This account of the Cincinnati encounter combines two renditions of the story, one by Gaylord Donnelley, in Donnelley Interview, and one by Zimmerman (ibid., 2). The quotation is from Zimmerman, who implies that he heard it personally from Reuben Donnelley in 1906.

15. The nickname "Ted" was derived from Thomas Elliott Donnelley's initials. This portrait of the brothers is based primarily on the Donnelley interview and on Gaylord Donnelley's letter to David G. Allen (November 1, 1985), hereafter cited as Donnelley Letter.

16. The story about the differing versions of a shared encounter is told both by Gaylord Donnelley (Donnelley interview) and by H. P. Zimmerman, who worked with the Donnelley brothers in these years. Cf. Zimmerman, "Donnelley and the Telephone Company, Part II," 1.

17. Zimmerman, "Donnelley and the Telephone Company, Part I: 1886-1906," 27.

18. This letter, to James H. Brundage, is reproduced in the folder titled "Letterheads," under Miscellaneous.

19. Zimmerman, "Donnelley and the Telephone Company," I, 27; II, Supplement, 1-2. Zimmerman took over Alexander Loyd's position as a kind of sales manager or customer service representative in 1902 and was very much involved in the expansion of Donnelley's directory printing in this period.

20. Ibid., I, 15; and II, Supplement, 3-8.

21. Ibid., II, Supplement, 2-3.

22. The employee is Donnelley's famous Abe Epstein, who stayed with the firm for well over 50 years. He is quoted here in ibid., II, Supplement, 17-18.

23. Ibid., II, Supplement, 2, 19-20, 28-30; and Nelson Letter.

NOTES TO CHAPTER III

1. Zimmerman "Donnelley and the Telephone Company," I, 28-32, and II, 8-9.

2. On *The National Classified Telephone Directory*, S. A. Welshans, "History of the Reuben H. Donnelley Corporation" (Unpublished MSS, 1951, filed under various dates in Hist. Info. File). Financial information from the Reuben H. Donnelley Corporation's file of its Board of Directors Meeting Minutes, maintained at corporate headquarters, Purchase, New York, Vol. 1, 35-38 (hereafter cited by volume as Board Minutes). The figure cited for Donnelley's assets is net. In 1917, he calculated his gross income from directories to be about $379,000.

3. Four years later, in 1921, the Chicago Directory Company would rise again, briefly, as Donnelley tested the waters for buyers of a revived city directory. But "the Chicago Directory Company" officially determined at that time that not enough people would subscribe to make a going venture, and so the scheme was dropped, ending the brief second life of the Chicago Directory Company. In 1924, there were nine employees who could celebrate with "R. H." service to the company going back into the 19th century—one all the way back to 1885—and probably many more who made the transition in 1917 but who had not been with Donnelley long enough to make the Twenty-Five Year Club, which he started in that year.

4. Board Minutes, I, n.p., Board of Directors meeting, December 15, 1919.

5. An advertising flyer for *Donelley's Industrial Directory* can be found in Hist. Info. File (1923).

6. *Lakeside Press Magazine* (April, 1923), 30.

7. In the language of marketing specialists of the 1980s, "[t]his early creative use of data to target emerging consumer segments is an example of the Donnelley philosophy of having the right information and putting that information to work." Quoted from "Donnelley Marketing History," a document produced by Donnelley Marketing for internal use, n.d.

8. *The Lakeside Press Magazine* (June, 1921), 31.

9. Reuben Donnelley's opinions on his visit to Nevada are from Gaylord Donnelley (interview, January 15, 1985). On the early growth of the M & F Mailing System, *The Nevada Evening Journal*, n.d., 1921, in "Nevada Iowa R.H.D., 50th Anniversary" (May, 1972). A copy of this commemorative document was given to me by Edward P. Harrington, Vice President of Donnelley Marketing.

10. *Lakeside Press Magazine* (April, 1923), 29.

11. This paragraph and the next are based on numerous news clippings in Hist. Info. File (1920); Donnelley's involvement in the Better Business Bureau was brought to my attention by Edward Harrington.

12. The quotation is from Donnelley's Christmas message in *The Lakeside Press Magazine* (December, 1922), 3.

13. Donnelley Interview and *The Lakeside Press Magazine*, passim. The Donnelley's lost a third, younger brother, Benjamin Donnelley, in 1922 (Donnelley genealogy, maintained with Hist. Info. File).

14. Donnelley Interview; Zimmerman, II, Supplement, 20, 30.

15. Abe Epstein's account is quoted in Zimmerman, II, Supplement, 18. The characterization of the Chicago office and the "rough-and-tumble" atmosphere of the business in these days is based on an interview with Donald R. Arnold, former President of The Reuben H. Donnelley Directory Company, in Atherton, California, February 11, 1985 (hereafter cited as Arnold Interview).

16. The preceeding two paragraphs and quotations are from "Highlights of the talk given by Mr. J. Morgan Jones, the General Directory Sales Manager, at the January meeting of the Chicago Department Heads and their assistants," in *Lakeside Press Magazine* (February, 1924), 27.

17. Donnelley's talk is quoted in *The Lakeside Press Magazine* (June, 1922), 28.

18. These quotations are from the Milwaukee and Baraboo directories, reproduced in Zimmerman, II, 5A, 6A.

NOTES TO CHAPTER IV

1. Telephone statistics are from *Historical Statistics of the U.S*, Part II, Series R 1-12, 783.

2. Retail sales and general directory statistics are from "History and Growth of Telephone Directory Advertising," Reuben H. Donnelley, Standard Reference, Part 2-B (n. d., but probably written by Milton W. Berriman in the early 1950s), 8. Donnelley statistics from "Comparative Profit and Loss Before Federal Income Tax—By Office," in J. C. Walker, comp., "Historical Statistics" (January 26, 1962).

3. "History and Growth of Telephone Directory Advertising," 4-6, 8-9.

4. *The Lakeside Press Magazine* (March, 1930), 31; "History and Growth of Telephone Directory Advertising," 9.

5. This portrait is based largely on the Arnold Interview.

6. This and the following paragraph are based on the Arnold Interview and an interview with Evert F. Nelson, former Vice President of Chesapeake and Potomac Region, in Rockville, Maryland, January 22, 1985 (hereafter cited as Nelson Interview).

7. American Telephone and Telegraph Company, Department of Operation and Engineering, *Directory Advertising Sales Training Manual* (New York, 1932).

8. The Reuben H. Donnelley Corporation, *The Donnelley Manual of Directory Salesmanship* (Chicago, 1934). Recollections of the introduction of the book are from the Arnold and the Nelson Interviews.

9. Epstein's reminiscences are in New York Region *Round Up* (January, 1959), n.p.; on AT&T and the sale of National Trade Marks, "History and Growth of Telephone Directory Advertising," 6.

10. These early sales aids were recovered through the Reuben H. Donnelley Centennial Contest. "Selling the Eye as Well as the Ear," was submitted by Thomas J. Stevens, Sr.; and "The Road to the Invisible Market," was submitted by Rae Mervis.

11. Evert F. ("Moose") Nelson was Sales Observer for Illinois, Christopher Porter for Pennsylvania, and Milton Berriman one of the two for New York (Nelson Letter).

12. This and the following paragraph are based on the Arnold Interview; the Nelson Interview; an interview with William W. Geary, former Vice President of Illinois-Cincinnati Region, in Chicago, January 7–8, 1985 (hereafter cited as Geary Interview); and an interview with Kenneth O. Johnson, President of Donnelley Directory, May 16, 1985 (hereafter cited as K. O. Johnson Interview). *The Donnelley Advertiser* was the brainchild of Don Arnold and Moose Nelson and was an internal publication of the Illinois state and suburban area that was distributed also to company officers and to managers in the Chicago sales organization (Nelson Letter).

13. The memoir of Joe Silverberg is from Donnelley employee Edward Secote. The characterization of the New York region under Gunnison is based largely on an interview with Curtiss E. Frank, former President of the Dun & Bradstreet Corporation, in New York, January 17, 1985 (hereafter cited as Frank Interview); and Arnold Interview.

14. This paragraph and the next are based on the Arnold Interview; the Nelson Interview; an interview with Morton C. Pry, former Vice President of Chesapeake and Potomac Region, in Rockville, Maryland, January 22, 1985 (hereafter cited as Pry Interview); and Board Minutes, XVI, 3095.

15. Revenue and profit statistics are from J. C. Walker, comp., "Historical Statistics," under "Telephone Directory Division."

16. Board Minutes, VI, 1108; and Frank Interview.

17. Board Minutes, VI, 1218-1221.

18. This paragraph and the next are based on Board Minutes, VI, 1217; and Frank Interview.

19. Arnold Interview; an interview with William L. Johnson, former President and Chairman of The Reuben H. Donnelley Corporation, in Delray, Florida, February 6, 1985 (hereafter cited as W. L. Johnson Interview); and the reminiscences of Edith Robinson and Ethel McGrath, submitted to the Donnelley Centennial Contest.

20. W. L. Johnson interview and an interview with LaRue G. ("Buck") Buchanan, former Senior Vice President, Reuben H. Donnelley Corporation. Statistics on retail sales are from *U. S. News and World Report,* cited in Reuben H. Donnelley Corporation, "Sales Round-Up," Penn-Delaware Division, II:1 (January, 1953), n.p.

21. Board Minutes, VI, 1112.

22. Board Minutes, VIII, 1533; and IX, 1736.

23. Board Minutes, IX, 1736-1737; XI, 3163-3164.

24. This paragraph and the next are based on the Nelson, W. L. Johnson, and Pry interviews.

NOTES TO CHAPTER V

1. Frank Interview; Board Minutes, X, 1893-1896, and XII, 2165; and Hist. Info. File (1951).

2. I am grateful to Jan Cremer, of the Mid-Atlantic Region, and Grace Langan, of the Mid-West Region, for making available to me back issues of their "Round-Ups" and other regional publications.

3. Board Minutes, XV, 2787.

4. Board Minutes, XIV, 2538.

5. On O'Rorke, see "Head Office Briefs" (September, 1953), 3; on management programs, Board Minutes, XVI, 3021; and XVIII, 3360.

6. Board Minutes, XIX, 3618.

7. Board Minutes, XII, 2166-2167; and Frank Interview.

8. Board Minutes, XII, 2166, and XIV, 2534; and Frank Interview.

9. The quotations are from Board Minutes, XIV, 2537, and XV, 2730. Other sources are Board Minutes, X, 1893; XV, 2823; and Frank Interview. The young engineer, Charles Lake, went on to be President and Chairman of R. R. Donnelley & Sons. He remembers that when Elliott Donnelley appeared in New York to see how things were going, he was immediately put to work processing orders (Donnelley Letter).

10. Board Minutes, XIV, 2537; XV, 2778, 2824; XVI, 3023, 3051; and Frank Interview.

11. Board Minutes, XVI, 3023, 3164.

12. The quotation is from Board Minutes, XVIII, 3418-3419. Bell System revenue statistics are from *The Round Up*, Pennsylvania–Delaware Region, 7:5 (May–June, 1956), 5. Also, Board Minutes, XV, 2827; XIX, 3618-3619, 3678; Arnold Interview.

13. Board Minutes, XVI, 3160; *The Round-Up*, Pennsylvania-Delaware Region, 3:8 (October, 1954), 2; and 4:1 (January, 1955), 5; *The Round-Up*, New York Region (May, 1958), n.p.; *The Round-Up*, Illinois-Cincinnati Region, 4:9 (April, 1956), cover; Arnold and Geary interviews.

14. Board Minutes, XXI, 4038; XXII, 4117, 4258; XXIII, 4409-4410, 4433, XXIV, 4617; and "Head Office Briefs" (n.d., 1956).

15. Board Minutes, XVI, 3025, 3160; *Sales Round-Up*, Pennsylvania-Delaware Region (Christmas Issue, 1953), n.p.; Hist. Info. File (1957).

16. Pry Interview.

17. Board Minutes, XXII, 4338.

18. Arnold Interview; Board Minutes, XII, 4119, 4258; XXIII, 4334, 4409-4410; XXIV, 4535, 4590-4591, 4619; XXV, n.p. (President's Report, March 1, 1961, 3).

19. *This is Donnelley's: The Story of the Reuben H. Donnelley Corporation* (Chicago: Reuben H. Donnelley, 1955), 33-41; Board Minutes, XIV, 1307; XV, 2784; XIX, 1737.

20. This paragraph is based on a profile of "Ham" Mitchell in "Head Office Briefs," n.d., n.p. (ca. 1954); Board Minutes, XXIV, 4539; and an Interview with Harrington E. Drake, Jr., former Chairman of Dun & Bradstreet Companies, Inc., in New York, June 18, 1985 (hereafter cited as Drake Interview).

21. *This is Donnelley's* and Board Minutes, VII, 1221; XIV, 1307; XVII, 3623.

22. Board Minutes, XXIII, 4433.

23. Charles C. Haffner, Jr., letter to David L. Harrington (May 16, 1960), in Hist. Info. File.

24. Ibid.

25. Thorne Donnelley obituary, *New York Times* (April 25, 1963), 33:2; Nelson Interview; Frank Interview.

26. "The Dun & Bradstreet Corporation History," (internal information sheet, maintained with Hist. Info. File); and James D. Norris, *R. G. Dun & Co., 1841-1900: The Development of Credit-Reporting in the Nineteenth Century*, Contributions in Economics and Economic History, Number 20 (Westport, Conn.: Greenwood Press, 1978), 86-87.

27. Frank Interview; Board Minutes, XXII, 4205.

28. Frank Interview, Drake Interview.

29. Quoted in *The Round-Up*, Pennsylvania-Delaware Region (Christmas, 1961), n.p., in Hist. Info. File (1961).

30. Frank Interview, Drake Interview.

NOTES TO CHAPTER VI

1. The quotation is from Board Minutes, XXIV, 4537.

2. Board Minutes, Series 2, Vol. I, President's Report (October 25, 1961), 5; and Vol. II, President's Report (January 17, 1962), 5. *Dateline Donnelley* (November–December, 1963), 7.

3. "Donnelley Marketing History," 2-3; Board Minutes, Series 2, Vol. III, President's Report (January 15, 1964), 3, 7.

4. Board Minutes, Series 2, Vol. II, President's Report (January 17, 1962), 3-4; and Vol. III, President's Report (January 16, 1963), 3-4.

5. This paragraph and the next are based on "Head Office Briefs" (September, 1953), n.p.; Board Minutes, Series 2, Vol. III, President's Report (March 20, 1963), 2; President's Report (July 17, 1963), 2; and President's Report (October 16, 1963), 3.

6. Board Minutes, Series 2, Vol. III, President's Report (October 16, 1963), 4; and President's Report (January 15, 1964), 3-4.

7. Board Minutes, Series 2, Vol. IV, Chairman's Annual Report (January 14, 1965), 3-4; W. L. Johnson Interview; and an interview with Richard B. Swank, Executive Vice President, Dun & Bradstreet Companies, Inc., in Purchase, N.Y., May 8, 1985 (Hereafter cited as Swank Interview).

8. W. L. Johnson Interview; Board Minutes, Series 2, Vol. IV, President's Report (January 20, 1965), 3.

9. Nelson Interview; W. L. Johnson Interview; and Position Descriptions (n.d.), Donnelley Archives, Spring Valley, N.Y.

10. Board Minutes, Series 2, Vol. VI, President's Report (January 13, 1967), 3; Pry Interview; W. L. Johnson Interview.

11. Nelson Interview; Pry Interview; W.L. Johnson Interview; Board Minutes, Series 2, Vol. VI, President's Report (January 13, 1967), 3.

12. Board Minutes, Series 2, Vol. V, Chairman's Report (January 10, 1966), 3-4; and President's Report (January 19, 1966), 4-5; Vol. VIII, President's Report (January 9, 1969), 4; Swank. Interview.

13. Cresap, McCormick and Paget, "The Reuben H. Donnelley Corporation Directory Division: Opportunities for Improvement in National Yellow Pages Service Operations," Consultants' Report (February, 1968); and "The Reuben H. Donnelley Corporation Directory Division: Opportunities for Improving Local Yellow Pages Marketing Services and Sales Promotion," Consulting Report (December, 1968).

14. Board Minutes, Series 2, Vol. VI, President's Report (January 13, 1967), 3-4; and VII, President's Report (March 20, 1968), 3, 6.

15. This paragraph and the next are based on Board Minutes, Series 2, Vol. VII, President's Report (March 20, 1968), 4; Swank Interview; and William Warren Lazarus, "The Yellow Pages: A Medium, An Industry" (Ph. D. diss., Massachusetts Institute of Technology, 1984), Chapters 5 and 8.

16. Board Minutes, Series 2, Vol. VIII, President's Report (January 9, 1969), 5; W. L. Johnson Interview; Swank Interview,; and Drake Interview.

17. *Who? What? Where?* (the regional publication of the Illinois/Cincinnati region, January-February, 1972), n.p.

18. Board Minutes, XXIII, 4332; W. L. Johnson Interview; Geary Interview.

19. *Dateline Donnelley* (July-August, 1971), 4-6; *Donnelley-Directory Record* 2 (1971), 3-4; Geary Interview.

20. The quotation is from Donald Brice, National Marketing Coordinator, in *Dateline Donnelley,* 1:2 (July-August, 1962), 6.

21. Drake Interview.

22. Harrington E. Drake, Jr., "Managing Change," A Presentation to the New York Society of Security Analysts (May 11, 1976), n.p.

23. Drake, "Managing Change;" Drake Interview; and Swank Interview.

24. W. L. Johnson Interview.

NOTES TO CHAPTER VII

1. "An Interview for the Record: Ed Hancharik," *Donnelley-Directory Record* (1979), No. 2, 9.

2. Ibid, 7-9; Lazarus, "The Yellow Pages," Chapter 6; Swank Interview.

3. "The 70's. A Decade of Growth for Independents," *Donnelley-Directory Record* (1979), No. 1, 5-9; and (1978), No. 2, 3, 4, 10; Pry Interview.

4. *Donnelley-Directory Record* (1971), No. 2, 21; *The Donnelley Record* (1981), No. 1, 15-17; and (1982), 4. [Note: the title of this publication changed in 1980, hence the use of two different names in these notes.] Swank Interview, W. L. Johnson Interview.

5. Project GO reports: "Workshop II, Strengthening Sales/Sales Management" (April 17, 1979), and "Summary of Major Opportunities and Recommended Actions" (June 6, 1979); Bak Interview.

6. *The Donnelley Record* (1980), No. 3, 4; and (1982), 3; and Bak Interview.

7. K. O. Johnson Interview.

8. The quotation is from Richard Swank in *The Donnelley Record* (1982), 3.

9. *The Donnelley Record* (1984), No. 1, 14-15; Swank Interview; Bak Interview; K. O. Johnson Interview; Drake Interview.

10. *The Donnelley Record* (1980), No. 2, 20; and (1982), 3.

11. *The Donnelley Record* (1985), No. 1, 1-5, 24; Swank Interview; Bak Interview; K. O. Johnson Interview.

DONNELLEY AND INDUSTRY
EXECUTIVES INTERVIEWED

Donald R. Arnold
  *Former President, Reuben H.
  Donnelley Directory Company*
William Bak
  *President, Donnelley Information
  Publishing*
LaRue G. Buchanan
  *Former Senior Vice President,
  Reuben H. Donnelley Corporation*
Michael J. Collins
  *Former Vice President and General
  Manager, Midwest Region, Reuben
  H. Donnelley Corporation*
Gaylord Donnelley
  *Former Chairman, R. R. Donnelley
  & Sons, Inc.*
Harrington E. Drake, Jr.
  *Former Chairman, Dun &
  Bradstreet Companies, Inc.*
Robert Edwards
  *Former Vice President, R. R.
  Donnelley & Sons, Inc.*
Raymond H. Eshelman
  President, L.M. Berry & Company
Curtiss E. Frank
  *Former President, Dun & Bradstreet
  Corporation*
William W. Geary
  *Former Vice President and General
  Manager, Illinois/Cincinnati Region,
  Reuben H. Donnelley Corporation*
Gary Garrison
  *Formerly of Directory Division,
  American Telephone & Telegraph
  Company*

Edward P. Harrington
  Vice President, Donnelley Marketing
Roger T. Hughes
  *Vice President & General Manager,
  Midwest Region, Donnelley
  Directory*
Kenneth O. Johnson
  President, Donnelley Directory
Ed Jordan
  *Former Executive Vice President,
  General Telephone Directory
  Company*
William L. Johnson
  *Former Chairman, Reuben H.
  Donnelley Corporation*
Malcolm W. McDonald
  *Former President, National
  Telephone Directory Corporation*
Hamilton B. Mitchell
  *Former Chairman, Dun &
  Bradstreet Corporation*
James Neaylon, Jr.
  *Marketing Manager, Donnelley
  Directory*
Evert F. Nelson
  *Former Vice President and General
  Manager, Chesapeake & Potomac
  Region, Reuben H. Donnelley
  Corporation*
Louis P. Pantaleo
  *Senior Vice President, Donnelley
  Information Publishing*

Morton C. Pry
Former Vice President and General Manager, Chesapeake & Potomac Region, Reuben H. Donnelley Corporation

Fred E. Smykla
Executive Director, National Yellow Pages Service Association

Richard B. Swank
Executive Vice President, The Dun & Bradstreet Corporation

Charles J. Wielgus
Executive Vice President, Human Resources and Communications, The Dun & Bradstreet Corporation